An ABC Primer for Church Musicians

An ABC Primer for Church Musicians

Bob Burroughs

BROADMAN PRESS
Nashville, Tennessee

© Copyright 1990 • Broadman Press
All rights reserved
4233-07
ISBN: 0-8054-3307-4
Dewey Decimal Classification: 780
Subject Heading: CHURCH MUSIC // MINISTERS OF MUSIC
Library of Congress Catalog Card Number: 89-17424
Printed in the United States of America

Unless otherwise indicated, Scripture quotations are from the *New American Standard Bible.* © The Lockman Foundation, 1960, 1962, 1963, 1968, 1971, 1972, 1973, 1975, 1977. Used by permission. Scripture quotations marked (KJV) are from the *King James Version* of the Bible.

Library of Congress Cataloging-in-Publication Data
Burroughs, Bob, 1937-
    An ABC primer for church musicians / Bob Burroughs.
        p.   cm.
    ISBN 0-8054-3307-4
    1. Church music—Miscellanea.   I. Title.
ML3001.B93   1990   89-17424
781.71—dc20   CIP

Foreword

An ABC Primer for Church Musicians is an extremely valuable book. If you are a veteran minister of music, read slowly and your life will pass before your eyes. If you are just beginning, read carefully! It will save you a heap of trouble, heartache, frustration, and trial and error.

Bob Burroughs has done us all a favor in giving us the timely comments within this book. I recommend it highly to you.

JAMES D. WOODWARD
Shawnee, Oklahoma

Preface

An ABC Primer for Church Musicians is for music directors, accompanists, and other church musicians interested in directing choirs and working with musical responsibilities in a church.

This book is full of creative ideas and suggestions, statements that will cause you to smile and think, humor, and some surprises.

Having been in the local church ministry of music since 1956, I wish I had been given such a primer when I began. The years between then and now would have gone so much smoother! The *A-Z* items come from years of personal experience, encounters, committee meetings, pastors, staff, church members, choir members, and much more.

I would not trade those years for the joys that have come through these experiences. Nor would I trade the sorrows and tears, for all have been experiences of growth and maturing. Maybe *An ABC Primer* will make service a bit easier and more enjoyable for those who are involved in a local church music ministry.

I wish for you the joys that have been mine in the service of God, the Father.

CONTENTS

- A: Alto 11
- B: Basses 13
- C: Committees 15
- D: Day Off 18
- E: Energy 23
- F: Fatherhood 28
- G: Graded Choirs 32
- H: Higher Education 37
- I: Instrumentalists 42
- J: Janitor 48
- K: Keyboardists 51
- L: Laymen 56
- M: Motivation 60
- N: New vs. Old 64
- O: Officers 70
- P: Pastor/Staff 82
- Q: Quality 92
- R: Rehearsals 96
- S: Sopranos 103
- T: Tenors 106
- U: Unknown 109
- V: Visitation 112
- W: Worship 116
- X: X-tra Special 129
- Y: Yahweh 137
- Z: Omega 143

A
Alto

". . . a little lower . . ." (Ps. 8:5).

ALTOS . . . the lowest choral line that is normally sung by women. ALTOS . . . competitive with "that other section." ALTOS . . . usually very good choir members. The ALTOS will usually be the best sight-readers in a choir. They have had this skill sharpened by reading harmony for most of their singing career. ALTOS rarely get to sing the melody, and so, without even knowing it, they gradually become good readers—consistent readers.

ALTOS are the most willing to experiment, to try something new, to expand their vocal range up or down. Do not let them tell you they cannot sing in the upper register of the vocal line! They can, if challenged and encouraged. ALTOS can sing like second sopranos, but they tend to only want to sing those "good, old, low notes"—the lower the better! Some of the finest choral singing is captured in the ALTO line when it is in middle and upper ranges, well supported and the tone produced through the vocal mask. They can do it!

There is a certain charm about ALTOS that is infectious. They can spread this "germ" throughout the entire choir, and this is a good thing! Every choir should have people who bring humor, lightness, and charm to a rehearsal . . . and many times, the ALTOS do this.

Some people say that ALTOS keep messy choir folders. In the plastic pocket of the choir folder, one might find cough drops, cough drop wrapping paper (usually the noisy kind), tissue (normally used—and why they will save this is a mystery to all!). The following may also be found: candy bars (half eaten, of course), pencils (with no point), offering envelopes (empty), mints, and, once in a while, lace hankies (used, of course).

Other people have said that neither ALTOS nor the other section of women hang their choir robes neatly! If one judged neatness by the way ALTOS left their choir robes after a performance or a Sunday worship service, one would surely be embarrassed! Sleeves are tied up within the robe, the stole is half on-half off, and the robe is crooked on the hanger, but I don't believe any of this! One thing for sure—you can depend on ALTOS to get a job done! Assign it and, usually, it is completed—not without comment, but completed nevertheless. ALTOS are good workers, willing to go above-and-beyond the call of duty.

ALTOS need to be encouraged to sing a solo or join with someone for a duet. They usually won't do it without some encouragement. Singing a solo will help the ALTO grow in musicianship. Offer assistance. Offer to help select the music, to help in the rehearsal, and be "of good cheer"! And compliment them following the solo/duet; it will do wonders for their spirit and make them better choir members.

ALTOS . . . good sight-readers . . . good spirits . . . congenial. ALTOS . . . the second largest section by number. ALTOS make a good addition to any choir fellowship!

B
Basses

". . . He brings low . . ." (1 Sam. 2:7).

BASSES . . . the lowest choral line sung by men.
BASSES . . . the "real men who don't eat quiche."
BASSES love to sing low—the lower, the better! It doesn't make any difference if the sound that is emitted is like wind blowing over a soft drink bottle! BASSES want to sing low!

BASSES do not like to sing high. "High," of course, is relative. Middle C is too high; G (fourth space-bass clef) is "high enough" for any true bass, they will tell you . . . but . . . BASSES can and should sing in that upper register. BASSES should be able to sing E-flat-above-middle-C with no problem (except their own!). BASSES need to stretch their upper vocal register as well as their lower register. But they must be driven, made fun of, shown how, and cajoled to do it.

BASSES are usually the third largest section in the choir, next to sopranos and altos. Numbers vary, of course, due to the size of the choir. BASSES are important. BASSES add that wonderful depth to choral sound. BASSES give security to the other sections when they are secure in their notes and music.

BASSES tend to be older than the other choir members. Maybe this is because it takes longer for the voice to settle! Maybe this is because a "true bass" doesn't mature till the later years. But nevertheless, BASSES have a certain maturity about them that is wonderful—yet childlike.

Baritones have not been mentioned as yet . . . and this is a voice part that must be reckoned with! Baritone is the male voice that lies between tenor and bass. Someone has said, "Baritones combine the negative qualities of both Tenors and BASSES, and they have a tendency to sing a different piece of music than everyone else . . . and sound like a trombone filled with cold coffee." That isn't necessarily true! Some of the better singers in a choir will be the baritones . . . who can't reach the lower bass notes and don't care to reach the tenor notes . . . so they sing very well and content in their range . . . the middle. When there is not a baritone part, baritones usually sing parts of the bass and parts of the tenor . . . depending on which part is most comfortable to their limited range! Or . . . they make up their own part!

BASSES enjoy a good joke . . . a good cup of dark, roasted coffee . . . any mistake the director makes . . . writing funny things in their music . . . a new anthem with a "low" bass part . . . pulling off a funny surprise on someone . . . parties . . . and leaving their coffee cup under their seat (which is usually spilled before long.)

BASSES dislike being on committees . . . hanging up their robes neatly . . . high vocal lines . . . tenors in general . . . pushy people . . . singing solos (usually caused by not watching the director) . . . and long, self-indulgent closing prayers.

Long live the BASSES—the choir foundation!

C
Committees

"And working together with Him . . ." (2 Cor. 6:1).

COMMITTEES—church COMMITTEES—the very sound of these words sometimes brings "fear and trembling" to the hearts and minds of staff members! Every church seems to be "committee poor," meaning there are sometimes more COMMITTEES than purposes—or people. Some churches even manage to have a committee on COMMITTEES!

There are negative and positive comments to be made for church COMMITTEES. Staff members usually must work with whatever COMMITTEES are in place. They are the "Committee" and it shall be.

The "Gloria Patri" seems to be the national anthem of many churches and many committees: "As it was in the beginning . . . 'tis now . . . and ever shall be . . . world without end . . . Amen!"

The staff is called by the church to minister in their areas of expertise. Many times, COMMITTEES that are responsible in these same areas have no wish to receive any direction from the staff member responsible for those areas. This is amazing!

COMMITTEES are usually run by laypeople, and wise COMMITTEES will allow the staff member to have some input to the workings of these COMMITTEES and have the opportunity to "shed light" on the decisions that are made. These COMMITTEES are usually run by men and women who love the Lord and feel the committee is one of the avenues of service they can give to God. With some assistance from staff in training and carrying out of responsibilities, COMMITTEES can function quite well, taking much of the burden of responsibility from the shoulders of staff members, who are then free to do other things.

Sometimes COMMITTEES are controlled by certain individuals, who often circumvent the staff, the church, or the original intent of the committee . . . to have everything done their way. The committees become a "power source" for a tiny area of the church program. This presents a good challenge to staff leadership!

A good solution is to pray specifically for the committee and turn the committee over to the Lord. Let Him deal with it in His own quiet, gentle way.

A good rule of thumb for staff members is simply this: *Never* go up against a church member over the decision of a committee! No matter how angry one gets or how slanted the decisions of the committee, a staff member will lose every time when pitted against a church member. Don't try it—it is not worth the heartache or pain that will come from that encounter.

Simply back off and let go of it. It is beyond your control. All you can do is offer your suggestions, your input, your experience, your counsel . . . and then, the committee is free to do with that information what they think is in the best interest of the church and the program. It is out of your hands, is it not? So go as far as you can with the committee and/or the chairman . . . then give it to them for their decision and you go with the flow. You be happy either way the decision is made

Committees

... and you will be happier, healthier, and perhaps a bit more humble.

Many times there are just too many COMMITTEES, both in the church and in the choir. COMMITTEES sometimes overlap and get in each other's way.

While it is true that many churches and choirs have way too many COMMITTEES, there is a strong feeling that the more laypeople who are involved in the inner workings of the church via committee, the stronger church family you will have and the more interest will be shown in the church and her program.

This is true. People take a high interest in the things in which they are involved. So if you want to keep your people "tied in" to the church program, put them on COMMITTEES that fit their skills and let them work in those areas, eventually tying them in closer to the church.

This is also true of the choir. But the size of the choir will determine how many COMMITTEES you need... as well as the number of officers you need. This will be discussed later in detail under O—OFFICERS.

Active, healthy, and somewhat aggressive people are usually the ones named to chair committees. *Aggressive* here does not mean dominant or pushy. It means people who have a certain vitality about them, allowing leadership of people to a decision-making point that is beneficial to the church. If a committee is not functioning, it is not a committee. It needs to function for the purpose for which it was created or disband. This is good, too, for it puts pressure on each committee chairman to see that the committee stays active and reports to the church at least once per quarter in church conference.

COMMITTEES... excellent tools to use in assisting the staff and the church to utilize more people to do the ministry of the fellowship.

D
Day Off

"Rest in the Lord and wait patiently for Him" (Ps. 37:7).

DAY OFF . . . a day to slip down to the church for a little "catch-up" work. DAY OFF . . . a day to concentrate on some church work at home. DAY OFF . . . a time to make phone calls about the choir festival. DAY OFF . . . a day to draw plans for the revival. DAY OFF . . . a day to go to the book store and look for new music. DAY OFF . . . a day to catch up on visitation. DAY OFF . . . a day to do hospital calls. DAY OFF . . . a day to . . . a day to . . . a day to. . . .

No! No! No! A DAY OFF is a DAY OFF! It is *not* to be used for "catch-up" church work. It *is* to be used to restore your mind. It is a time to spend with your family, especially your spouse. It is a time to cut the grass, trim the roses, go fishing, play racquetball, work a crossword puzzle, go out to dinner. It is a time to step back from your daily responsibilities and a time to renew yourself. It is a time to play with the children . . . to find out what is going on in their lives. It is a time to do something for YOU.

The church office should not bother you on your DAY OFF, except in an emergency. The secretaries should not call your home for trivial things. Staff members should not bother other staff members on their DAY OFF! Church members should not bother staff members on their DAY OFF, although this one is rather difficult to control!

I speak from experience. I speak as one who rarely took his DAY OFF in those early years and who regrets it even to this day! But . . . I wanted to "be somebody," to achieve, to impress my church members with how dedicated I was and what a good minister I was because I was at the church day and night with ensembles, handbells, committee meetings, visiting, choir rehearsals, and on and on and on. I missed seeing my son and daughter grow up in their early years because I was "at church." I missed some grand experiences with my wife because I was "at church." It was not until my children were in junior high school that I came to my senses and began to spend quality time with them.

I discovered I could cook gourmet style, and my family loved my cooking as much as I loved doing it! I discovered I liked to do yard work. I discovered I liked to fish, although I wasn't very good at it and lost more lures than I caught fish. I discovered I liked to read—other things besides musical things.

I discovered my son could play racquetball and began playing with him almost every afternoon (he now beats me regularly). I discovered my son had musical abilities, so we had something in common to talk about while we were fishing, playing racquetball, or walking by the lake.

I discovered my daughter was a charming, humorous person who wrote wonderful things and wanted to share them with me. I discovered she admired me and loved me very much, but we couldn't find enough time to tell each other.

I discovered my wife had some wonderful gifts of

leadership. She was a creative, innovative person who had a way with people and was a person of worth in her own right and was not just the "wife of the minister of music." I discovered she enjoyed being with me as much as I was enjoying being with her. We both enjoyed getting the children to bed and having a late evening dinner—just the two of us—with our own special dinnerware!

But this delayed coming to my senses wasn't the fault of the church. It was my fault, too, because I would not take my DAY OFF and spend that time with my family and rest, relax, and refresh myself. You owe yourself your DAY OFF. You owe your family your DAY OFF. You owe your church this DAY OFF! You owe your secretary this DAY OFF! And no one can take this DAY OFF—but you!

Sunday is *not* your DAY OFF! Sunday is the most difficult day of the week for a staff member. It is literally dawn till midnight in most cases. It is the only time of the week when the largest body of the church family is gathered for worship and other things relating to Sunday. It is not a "day of rest" for staff members.

Your church should allow you a DAY OFF. On that DAY OFF, you need to "rest in the Lord" and "wait patiently for Him." You need to utilize that time for yourself, for your spouse, for your children, for your yard, for your physical well-being.

So many church staff members work seven days a week, with the example set by the pastor. "If I do it, you should do it too!" he says. If your pastor decides to grow old early because of tension, overwork, overachieving, overeating, no exercise, while building the "great church" and working up to a heart attack, that is no reason for the other staff to do it too! And . . . he should not require it of the other staff.

Some pastors put pressure on their staff to work beyond the hours that are required in a normal day's work. For instance, take Wednesdays—another important day. If the pastor requires all staff to be in the office by 8:30 or 9:00 a.m., most of the staff will be working a twelve- to fourteen-hour day.

This is certainly true of the music minister, who probably has adult choir rehearsal following the prayer service or Bible study. The rehearsal will probably be over by 9:00 p.m. By the time everyone is gone and the church is locked and secured, it is probably 9:30-10:00 p.m.—a fourteen-hour day. That is not a good way to be at your best, and it certainly leaves a lot lacking in your energy level!

All ministerial staff should be allowed to come in later on Wednesdays in order to compensate for the late evening responsibilities. Consider what a nice change of pace it would be for the ministerial staff to come to the office between 10:00-11:00 a.m., check in, do a few details, go to lunch, and have the afternoon to prepare for the evening's responsibilities.

The most important hour of the week for the music minister, besides Sunday morning, is the Wednesday night adult choir rehearsal. The music minister needs to be at his/her very best—top flight, raring to go, with ENERGY (to be discussed in a later chapter) abounding.

How can this happen if the music minister has been in the office since 8:30 a.m., visited the hospital(s), visited a new prospect, had staff meeting, had responsibility for the graded choirs, two handbell rehearsals, junior high choir, evening supper, and finally stumbles into adult choir rehearsal, frazzled, worn out, and weary— yet is expected to pull off a first-rate, exciting, energetic, musical and spiritual rehearsal? *This is impossible!* It will not work. Common sense dictates this.

If 8:30 a.m. is going to be required of ministerial staff, then a couple of hours should be allowed in the afternoon . . . to go home, put your feet up, stretch out for a few minutes, and relax before the late afternoon and evening begins. It will work wonders. And the program will be better in the long run because *freshness* will show up in the person, which will spill over into everything he/she touches the rest of the day.

D—DAY OFF . . . you must have it to keep in communication with your Creator, with your family, with yourself. Don't let it slip away from you. Of course, there will be occasions when your DAY OFF is eaten up by church responsibilities; but this should be rare, indeed!

My prayer and thought for you is that you learn this valuable lesson of the DAY OFF sooner than I did!

E
Energy

"He gives strength [ENERGY] to the weary,
and to him who lacks might [ENERGY], He increases
  power"
(Isa. 40:29).

ENERGY—a key to success with your choir, with your congregation, with your staff, with the committee. ENERGY—the one ingredient in education that cannot be taught. It must be learned . . . through experience.

Experts tell us that children give back 50 to 70 percent of the energy that is given to them by the teacher in a classroom situation. Then what percentage do you think your adults/youth will give back to you with the ENERGY that you give them in rehearsal? Suppose you only give about 75 percent on a given evening. You don't feel up to par. You've had a bad day. Then you can count on your choir giving back to you about 40 to 60 percent in return . . . and you will go home wondering why the rehearsal went so poorly!

I love to watch the "experts" work a rehearsal situation and see the ENERGY that is expended, the sweat that comes from the brow, the vitality that is given to the choir in order for the choir to return ENERGY to the conductor and, therefore, to the audience.

Mable Boyter, one of the premier children's choir leaders, is absolutely superb in rehearsals with children. She holds their attention from the time they enter the room till they are dismissed. No nonsense here, ladies and gentlemen! Just discipline—creative discipline that makes the children want to sing . . . to learn . . . to create music.

Then there is James D. Woodward, one of the premier conductors in the United States. His quiet, steady leadership inspires both choirs and directors! His ENERGY level is exhausting. And following a good two-hour rehearsal, he is "history"! He has expended all the energies in his body, mind, and spirit . . . but what a wonderful experience for the choir! They go home refreshed, awake, aware that they have truly made *music*.

Every time I am in a rehearsal or seminar with Woodward, I go home to my people a better conductor, more sensitive to the music. This comes from the amount of ENERGY expended in the rehearsal and the musicianship that is taught in a short time.

There are others who expend ENERGY and make rehearsals both fun and worthy of attendance. To name them all would be a "Hall of Fame" for high ENERGY levels . . . and you would find that their programs, be they in church or school, are successful due to their musicianship and their ability to work with people, to inspire people, to motivate people to be better than they are and to sing better than they are capable of singing because of their high ENERGY level.

How does one achieve this high ENERGY level for rehearsals, committee meetings, congregational experiences, and other activities? There is no set plan, no list of rules to follow, no guided tour into ENERGY.

Some commonsense things are worthy of note:
- *Exercise*—Daily and consistent exercise will give

one a higher ENERGY level. Walking two to three miles per day with your spouse will give some wonderful quality time to discuss today, tomorrow, the children, the church, whatever. Membership in the YMCA (YWCA) or a local health club or use of the church gym is a wonderful way to be consistent with an exercise program. Racquetball, weights, LifeCycle, tennis, basketball, or volleyball can add to your time spent to obtain more ENERGY. And exercise will prolong your life! Get that heart rate up there for a few minutes. Clean out those "pipes," and sweat a bit!

• *Foods*—have a great influence on your ENERGY level. I highly recommend *Fit for Life,* a book by Harvey and Marilyn Diamond (Warner Books). The foreword states that if you follow the recommendations of the book, you will lose weight, vastly increase your ENERGY from proper food combining, enjoy fruit, and discover a new life-style that will keep you slim and fit. The book will encourage you to exercise sanely, safely, and effectively and will change your way of eating. You will look and feel your best at all times! The book deals with the natural body cycle and contains excellent material.

You will be able to obtain ENERGY that you never have known before while eating the proper foods. Fruit is a wonderful ENERGY food.

• *Proper Rest*—is essential to a high ENERGY level, especially on rehearsal days! Remember: You can't go to work/church/school at 8:30 a.m. (or earlier), work all day, and expect to be in fit form or shipshape for the 7:30 p.m. rehearsal that evening without some rest to restore your ENERGY level. Some people require less sleep and/or rest than others; but on rehearsal days, you should obtain the proper amount of rest so you will be sharp, alert, and ready to meet the demands of a good, well-planned, and disciplined rehearsal.

- *Attitude*—is so important to your ENERGY level. You cannot fight with your spouse all morning and expect to be in any mental shape for a good rehearsal that evening. You can't wrestle with a committee and go into a rehearsal, expecting it to be full of excitement and ENERGY. Confrontations drain you mentally and physically.

Your attitude about rehearsal should be so intense that you purposely avoid any major confrontations before walking into that rehearsal. A confrontation will wait—and may work itself out . . . but don't waste good ENERGY in a confrontation when that ENERGY is needed in a demanding rehearsal.

- *Spiritual Strength*—will give you ENERGY. The Scriptures have direct references to *strength* and *might,* both of which can be translated "ENERGY."

> Psalm 28:7: "The Lord is my strength [ENERGY] and my shield."
>
> Psalm 46:1: "God is our refuge and strength " [ENERGY].
>
> Isaiah 40:29: "He gives strength [ENERGY] to the weary, and to him who lacks might [ENERGY], He increases power."
>
> 1 Peter 4:11: "By the 'strength' [ENERGY] which God supplies . . . ."

If your spiritual life is creative and innovative, if your walk with the Father of all life is regular and communication is open, you will find a new, abounding ENERGY in life itself. You can do rehearsals on your own strength for a while, but a certain ENERGY will be missing . . . the ENERGY provided you by the Holy Spirit, as you minister to your choir(s) through music and beyond: the interpretation of text, the wedding of text and music, the preparation for the performance ministry, and more.

The ENERGY you expend in rehearsal will come

back to you through the ENERGY the choir gives to you in response. This might not be a bad time for a personal checkup on yourself and your own ENERGY level.

F
Fatherhood

"I will be a Father to him,
and he shall be a Son to me"
(Heb. 1:5).

There is no greater calling in this world than FATHERHOOD (MOTHERHOOD). If you have chosen to have children, you have made the choice to be a father or mother to them.

Too often young couples, in all areas of ministry, commit to have children and then go off to "play church" and all but forget they have children. Children sometimes go for days without seeing father or mother.

Let's pretend. On a given Monday, there is a staff prayer breakfast at 7:30 a.m., so the church staff parent is up and gone before the children wake up! (The staff parent wants to give a good impression and be first at the breakfast, of course.) The day stretches on to lunch with a deacon, and before you know it handbell rehearsal is here, immediately following school. Then the youth ensemble takes the staff to the evening meal, which tonight is a church choir officers meeting at the president's home. It lasts beyond the appointed time, finishing at 9:00 p.m. On the way home, the staff parent makes one quick visit or hospital call and arrives home at 10:30 p.m., long past the bedtime of the children—and perhaps the spouse!

Tuesday arrives with a "pat on the head for the kids" as the staff parent is heading out the door for an 8:00 a.m. breakfast with the chairman of deacons. After a long, ministry-filled day and a late rehearsal with the adult ensemble, the staff parent arrives home at 10:00 p.m., just in time to scold the children for being awake at 10:00 p.m.—when they haven't seen him or her all day!

Then it is Wednesday. . . .

Sound familiar? It should because we have all been in that place at one time or another in our lives. Sometimes our children should call us "Uncle Daddy" because we "visit" them so seldom! Sometimes the church is responsible for this time of absence, requiring staff members to be certain places at times when FATHERHOOD is needed. And many times it is not really the "church"; it is the pastor who is doing the requiring.

Let us be practical here for a moment. There are but few times when a working father or working mother can be with children. Morning preparation and breakfast is one such time. Getting the children dressed and ready for school, sharing the breakfast table with them, and sharing a devotional thought together are important links to their spiritual and family growth.

After school is usually a time of play, homework, instrument lessons, sports, and who knows what else! Then there is supper—the most important meal of the day with the family. This meal is the time for everyone at the table to share with other members of the family what happened in their lives this day . . . a time of communication, a time of laughter, a time of good news, and a time of devotion together as a family.

Following dinner there is homework, practice, TV,

and getting ready for bed. Then the children are asleep and gone for the evening.

So just how much time is there to spend with your children? Ten minutes . . . more . . . or less? And before you know it, they have finished high school and are off to college. Then they are married and you are left with an empty nest . . . and you and your spouse have to get acquainted all over again.

The church (or pastor) does not have the right to consistently take you away from your children. They do not have the right to require early mornings and evenings of you on a regular basis. Of course, there will be times when this happens and it seems regular, but regular it should *not* become. You owe some quality time to your children and your spouse! They should not always get the "leftovers" of you, after a hard day's work, when you have nothing left to give. That is certainly not the least bit fair to your family, who loves you and deserves some time with you when you are fresh.

This is why your DAY OFF is important to you . . . and to your family! This is a day they can anticipate. This is a day when they can have a leisurely breakfast with Dad or Mom . . . Dad or Mom can take them to the bus or to school . . . Dad or Mom can meet them after school and go for an ice cream . . Dad or Mom can help with supper (or prepare it, perhaps with their assistance) . . . Dad or Mom can take them to the movies . . . Dad or Mom can give the children a bath! Of course, you would not do all these things every DAY OFF. You deserve some time reserved for you . . . but your children deserve some time from you too!

Give them quality time . . . it is much more important than quantity time!

One last word: Make sure your spouse has a large portion of your best times. Do not make the mistake of ministering to everyone in the church or school but never to your spouse. Do not be "married" to your spouse *and* to your church/school. This will not work and will end in heartbreak for all involved!

Plan some special times with your spouse. Surprises are wonderful. Picnics in the park are wonderful. Shopping is a wonderful therapy—just getting together, having lunch, and seeing the sights. A couple of days away is a good idea every so often. Fixing your favorite meal for the family is nice, or having a quiet, relaxed dinner with just the two of you.

FATHERHOOD (MOTHERHOOD)—a high priority for you, the father (mother)/minister/musician. Don't take it lightly. It is far too important, for you and for them.

G
Graded Choirs

"Train up a child in the way he should go . . ." (Prov. 22:6).

GRADED CHOIRS—the best training in music that is available for children through grade six. GRADED CHOIRS—the program where children learn musical skills, biblical truths, and the early basics of choral singing. GRADED CHOIRS—a wonderful enlistment program for children in the community.

GRADED CHOIRS—was that ever a good idea! Whoever was responsible for the concept that the church could provide quality music education to children through grade six, couple it with a biblical base, enlist and train the sharpest workers available, and share this with both the church family and the community should have a statue erected in his/her honor!

There isn't a finer program today than GRADED CHOIRS, and most churches have some kind of quality program for children through the sixth grade that teaches the musical skills necessary for a good beginning. A child who has gone through such a program will certainly be a leader in music through his junior high and high school years and on to adult choir!

More work and expense probably go into the preparation of materials for GRADED CHOIRS than any other single program of production. These materials are first-rate, first-class, well done, and at the top of the list. The best people are enlisted to dream and implement those dreams. The best composers write music for these children. The level of instruction is the best available anywhere.

Almost every denomination has a GRADED CHOIR program of some kind available on the public market. If not, excellent materials are available from the Church Music Department, Southern Baptist Sunday School Board, Nashville, Tennessee. These programs have tried-and-true materials that have been available since the 1950s. You may want to check with your local Christian book store for materials available from other publishers.

Sad to say, quality music education is no longer taught in our public schools. You will find some pockets of progress; but for the most part theory, band, and choral music have fallen by the wayside in favor of math, science, and other non-art classes. Children may have a music class once every two weeks, if that. You cannot expect much to be taught in such a classroom situation.

The local church, then, becomes the major supplier of music education for the community. If music and music education is going to be taught, it can be taught in the local church, through a GRADED CHOIR program.

What a wonderful opportunity is ours! What an opportunity to share the witness of the Father to our community through a quality music education program!

But a GRADED CHOIR program does not just happen because the church decides to begin one! Starting such a program requires enlistment, promotion, materials, and more.

The music minister may wish to direct one or more of these choirs, if this is an interest to him/her. But the music minister should not become the only GRADED CHOIR worker! Many times a music minister will direct several choirs, literally working himself to the bone. And when this musician leaves, the program stops. This is wrong! This is a self-indulgent ministry of music!

A music minister should multiply himself/herself again and again as he/she trains workers to be active in the music program. The more directors who are trained to direct the choirs, the stronger the music ministry will be as the music minister oversees the program.

Summer is the best time to train workers for the coming year. Several major conferences are available throughout the USA that will train your people in specific areas of music ministry and GRADED CHOIRS. Many states have training programs for GRADED CHOIRS. *Creator* Magazine (P. O. Box 100, Dublin, OH.) always lists the coming seminars in the spring issue of this monthly magazine. Every music minister should have a subscription to this excellent publication.

You can also have your own training program over a weekend in your church situation. Many times this is best, for you can tailor the instruction to fit your church program. You can enlist people from your community or nearby communities to help you train your workers.

If you are beginning a new program, a checklist of equipment is necessary. You have to have certain materials before you can begin to minister to children. The purpose of this book is not to give a detailed discussion of GRADED CHOIRS, but to simply give you an idea of what is involved with GRADED CHOIRS. You will find ample sources that give you detailed outlines of necessary equipment and materials, depending on what your budget can afford.

The next step is enlisting the staff. For each choir, you will need a director, a pianist, and a worker or two, depending on the size of the choir. You will obviously need more workers as the size of a choir increases.

Your directors should be good musicians, with personalities that win children's affection. They should be willing to work hard at this task and not take for granted that it will run itself. Much work is involved in having a good GRADED CHOIR program.

Your pianist(s) should be capable of playing the materials, willing to assist with the other activities of the rehearsal and to be a helper to the director. The other workers need to have an understanding of music and ministry to children and to be willing to give this time weekly to the children.

GRADED CHOIRS are not performance choirs! Grades 4-6 can perform three or four times per year, but not on a regular basis. Younger children should not be encouraged to sing on a regular basis, and not at all if you can get away with it! The large room, the "millions of adults," the lights, the smiling faces, and the pastor— all this intimidates children, and you will not get the best from the choir in this situation. Yet we do it year after year and we get a lot of waving at Mommy, stumbling on purpose for a laugh, and soft singing because of the difference in size from the rehearsal room to the sanctuary or fellowship hall.

Music ministers are sometimes pressured to let the children's choirs sing to "draw a crowd." If the children sing, the parents and grandparents will come and a large, ready-made audience will be there to hear the preaching. *This is wrong.* This is using the children to satisfy someone's ego. One uses things . . . not people.

This kind of ministry will succeed for the moment but will lose in the end.

I know churches that require all the GRADED CHOIRS to robe up every Wednesday following their rehearsals and sit together in the sanctuary for midweek Bible study. Each choir sings once per month. Sure, you have a room full of children, plus parents and other adults; and the numbers really look good for Wednesday night prayer meeting. I feel that the GRADED CHOIRS should not be used in this manner. To require the whole GRADED CHOIR program to be in prayer meeting is not only using the children but also could have the appearance of pressure to push the children to make spiritual decisions prematurely. The music minister should do all within his power to keep this from happening. It is not healthy for the children.

The GRADED CHOIR program can be a boon to your church, your community, and your people, as more and more children are involved and trained. Then at their own time, with careful counsel, the children can make decisions for Christ that will be true and honest.

I support GRADED CHOIRS, their workers, the program, the composers and writers of the curriculum, and the churches that support this wonderful ministry. Hats off to you!

H
Higher Education

"Study to shew thyself approved unto God . . ." (2 Tim. 2:15, KJV).

HIGHER EDUCATION is essential for all ministers, whether their area be music, preaching, youth, education, or children. HIGHER EDUCATION broadens the scope of your vision. HIGHER EDUCATION broadens your outlook on life. HIGHER EDUCATION provides you with learned skills and the honing of natural skills that will make you a better musician and a disciplined minister. HIGHER EDUCATION stretches you and your musical skills, makes you more confident, and gives you a chance to see beyond yourself.

You are never too old to learn something new. The old saying that "you can't teach an old dog new tricks" is simply not true. There is a certain magic and renewal to the personal spirit when one learns something new, exciting, and useful.

One of the pitfalls concerning HIGHER EDUCATION for young church musicians is the decision of whether to go for an advanced degree. One has just finished four years of high school, followed by four/five hard years in college obtaining a degree. One is weary of school, tired of studying. A nice church situation comes along and entices this young musician to be the minister of music and offers a very good salary . . . or at least it seems good at the time.

The young minister marries in the first year or two, works hard in the church, has a baby or two, and some increase in salary. Roots are developed and before you know it, this one is approaching thirty with only a bachelor's degree. His peers have gone on to graduate school, obtained their degrees, and are having wonderful opportunities come their way . . . while this one remains in a small local church, with little or no hope for change to something better or much higher salary—due to lack of education.

This scenario has been repeated time and time again. The money looks great immediately after college. The church is a nice size, ready for growth. The music program is attractive. But there comes a point when the lack of a higher degree limits the amount of money to be made and the further growth of music skills. The musician is frustrated to the point where he/she finally quits and goes into insurance, the old "stand-by," in order to make a little more money to support the family. Frustrations abound!

It doesn't always work this way. Around age twenty-seven or twenty-nine, some realize that there is more out there to be obtained with a higher degree and go on to secure a master's degree—even with a small family to support. They make it work for them.

And there is a small number who succeed without a higher degree. These are few and far between . . . and if you know some of these, you will discover they are usually resourceful in their ministries . . . always looking for new and creative ideas . . . seeking clinics and seminars to attend, satisfying the desire to seek HIGHER EDUCATION . . . and usually have good personalities.

They are well loved by their church family, who support them and see that they are provided more than the basics of life.

One of the good things happening in some local churches is the program of a sabbatical leave for staff members. Some churches allow a staff member to have three months off for HIGHER EDUCATION after three to five years of service. As the years increase, the time away increases too.

Whether or not a sabbatical leave is granted, some music ministers use vacation and/or time away during the summer to study and train. Some go to seminars across the land to meet their specific needs. Others go to a local college or university and obtain a special study program on an individual basis. Some travel overseas to study.

Many colleges/universities and some seminaries offer a four- to six-week refresher course in the summer or in the January Term for music ministers. These are usually excellent and offer a variety of courses for personal study.

All of the Southern Baptist theological seminaries offer seminars during the year on music and worship and refresher courses. Seminaries, colleges, and universities of other denominations also have seminars based along the same guidelines.

The Christian Artists Seminar, Estes Park, Colorado, in early August, is one of the outstanding seminars in the USA. The music minister can upgrade his own personal music skills in a variety of areas with the top music personalities in the country today—and rub shoulders with the most popular contemporary artists, producers, and performers at the same time! This seminar also makes a wonderful family event.

Churches that offer sabbatical leaves or other time off for educational purposes are the richer for it. They receive the direct benefit of the educational process. Every church should allow staff some time away for personal growth and HIGHER EDUCATION.

When one stops learning, searching, and discovering, one stops growing. Those music ministers who do the same set of anthems year after year are betraying their churches and themselves. Those music ministers who are always seeking new literature that will challenge their conducting skills and challenge the choir are the ministers who still have exciting and vital programs.

I do not believe that when a minister turns forty-five or fifty, he is ready to be "let out to pasture" and begin semiretirement! If one keeps up to date, one will stay informed and active in today's music circles. To say that a church won't look at someone age fifty-two is an indication that the church has had experience with someone of fifty-two in the past who had finished learning, growing, and stretching—and the program became boring. A person in his or her fifties can still relate to a congregation, to the church choir, and, yes—even to the youth choir! But many fifty-two-year-olds forget how to play, to laugh, to enjoy youth. That is why they don't "relate"! I know many directors who are over fifty and who have active, exciting programs—who still relate to children, youth, young adults, and adults . . . who still seek HIGHER EDUCATION to sharpen their skills . . . who won't let advancing age dim their outlook on life!

If you feel you aren't growing and relating, get away for a time! Rethink your priorities, your calling, and your ministry. Ask your church for a sabbatical leave to renew your music skills . . . to seek a fresh approach to ministry . . . to have the opportunity to begin again. Search for new ideas and new techniques that will challenge you and get the gray matter working in your head. Look for a challenge with your youth. Find a way to relate to them. Freshen up a bit! Maybe you are becoming old-fashioned because of your clothing or your hair (or lack of it). Turn these into assets! Life can work for you if you will work life! We should live life to the fullest, and we should not be retired at fifty. God did not intend for music ministers to become ineffective at any age! Ineffectiveness creeps up on you like a cancer. It makes you lose the challenge of life, the excitement of ministry, the aroma of success following a hard, disciplined choir rehearsal!

Don't ever let go of HIGHER EDUCATION! Keep learning. Keep growing. Keep challenging yourself to create, to be different, to be fresh, to be innovative in your ministry.

Your whole attitude will change. You will sense a new excitement in your spirit and soul. You will see a change in the way you conduct rehearsals and the energy you have for the worship services. It can happen to you!

I
Instrumentalists

"Shout joyfully to the Lord, all the earth;
Break forth and sing for joy and sing praises.
Sing praises to the Lord with the lyre;
With the lyre and the sound of melody.
With trumpets and the sound of the horn
Shout joyfully before the King, the Lord"
(Ps. 98:4-6).

INSTRUMENTALISTS add such an excitement and celebration to any worship service or special program. INSTRUMENTALISTS add that certain charm that enhances the anthem, the soloist, the prelude. INSTRUMENTALISTS usually charge!

Some of the most memorable worship experiences probably have been those in which INSTRUMENTALISTS were involved. The use of an orchestra with the Christmas music . . . the brass quartet with the anthem . . . the flute with the handbells . . . the harp with the children . . . instruments with the congregational singing . . . all of these and more create a wonderful sense of fulfillment for the choir, the congregation, and the director.

But some of the most embarrassing moments have also included INSTRUMENTALISTS. The early entrance of the first trumpet which threw everyone off,

Instrumentalists

never to regain their confidence . . . the temperamental flutist who walked out of rehearsal . . . the dropped handbell in the quiet section of the anthem . . . the out-of-tune strings in the cantata . . . the oboist who must have been playing the wrong end . . . all these and more create feelings of "never again"!

Here are some personal experiences regarding INSTRUMENTALISTS that might help you in the future:

- Become familiar with the instruments you are going to use and what is required to play them. It behooves you as a conductor to know what sounds to expect from your players. You do not have to actually know how to play an instrument to conduct instrumental players, but you must be familiar with the instrument and the sound produced.

- Secure INSTRUMENTALISTS well in advance of the program. This will ensure getting the better players.

- Provide INSTRUMENTALISTS with the music score well in advance of the program. They may or may not look at it, but at least they have been given the opportunity to see it in advance. Be sure to mark any problem spots, key changes, or tempo changes that might cause problems in the rehearsal.

- Give the INSTRUMENTALISTS ample time to warm up their instruments before the downbeat. INSTRUMENTALISTS and their instruments are sometimes temperamental, and a bit of extra time will help both.

- As the conductor, know the instrumental part well, so you can discuss it intelligently when problems arise. You are the conductor, and the instrumentalist is to play under your direction. So be sure you can call attention to accidentals and dynamics and can give the INSTRUMENTALISTS a sense of leadership. If not, a secure instrumentalist will lead you—and you do not want this!

- If the INSTRUMENTALISTS are nonprofessional, chances are they will have at least rehearsed the notes, meaning they may have gone through the part a couple of times. (Probably once!) If they have a band director or someone who will push them, they may come to rehearsal with their parts learned. If the INSTRUMENTALISTS are professional, chances are they will not have even gone through the score—especially if it is a familiar one, such as *Messiah*. They figure they are professionals and do not need to spend any time on it. This is not a good attitude, by the way!

If the INSTRUMENTALISTS come to the rehearsal with their part not secure, you have a choice of (1) canceling the use of their services, (2) discussing a lower fee than you contracted to pay them, or (3) getting a pledge from them that they will have the part learned by performance time. None of these choices are good, for it makes you the "bad guy" and will create tension. In essence, you can't win here. If the group is a "contract" group, discuss the problem with the "contractor" and let him deal with the problem. If the group is a "pick-up" group from the community, deal with the problem person privately, individually, so as not to cause embarrassment.

The obvious answer is to contract with people you know, in whom you have confidence, and whom you have used previously. Only then can you be certain of the caliber of performance.

- If the INSTRUMENTALISTS are to be paid, have their checks ready in advance. Don't make them wait. Secure their checks ahead of time and have them on their stands at the performance time.
- It is a good public relations gesture to pay anyone who is not a member of your church family. The

amount should be agreed upon by both parties prior to playing. It seems a bit much to expect a non-church member to learn a piece, rehearse it, and play it for just a nice "Thank you." If you can afford professional players in your budget, fine! If not, you are going to have to be content with the average or better-than-average players and the high school band or local college program.

- Utilize local players as often as possible, especially those within your own church program. This is a great way to grow your own instrumental program. Let them play as often as possible for worship services, senior citizens, youth, banquets, and the like. Find creative ways to involve these players in your program. Write parts for them to go with an anthem. Write descants for them to play on hymns. INSTRUMENTALISTS do not like to practice, practice, practice, and play! They like to practice and then play—practice and then play! Schedule them in often and well in advance, so they will know when and what they are to play.

- Do not let INSTRUMENTALISTS intimidate you—and they surely can do that. If there is anything worse than a "snooty" instrumentalist, it would be a "snooty" conductor. Many INSTRUMENTALISTS tend to radiate superior musicianship. This is certainly not true in every case. There are some delightfully gentle and easy-going INSTRUMENTALISTS. But if you, as conductor and director, are prepared, know your score, know their score, know what you want, and know what to expect of them, you will do just fine. Just do not allow yourself to be intimidated! You can do it!

- If you do not feel comfortable conducting, contracting, writing for, or dealing with INSTRUMENTALISTS, you can certainly turn this responsibility over to someone in your program who is comfortable doing this kind of work. Many music ministers allow someone else to conduct the instrumental program and the handbells. This is good, for it allows the music minister to use other people. And when he/she is gone, the program continues!

• Speaking of handbells, they count as instruments and some word should be said here about them. If handbells are not familiar or comfortable to you, you can allow others to conduct the group(s).

I started a handbell choir in 1966, when a five-octave set of Petit & Fritzen Handbells were discovered in the belfry of First Baptist Church, Abilene, Texas. The former minister of music didn't like bells; and when this five-octave set was given, he put them away and never used them. In 1966 not much handbell music was being published. There were only two handbell books, to my knowledge, both from H. W. Gray Company and both used extensively in the few churches/schools that had handbells. So we wrote and arranged music for handbells for our services out of self-defense!

I knew nothing about handbells—period! I didn't take any courses in college or graduate school that even mentioned handbells because none were offered! So anything I learned about handbells had to come from first-hand experience. We ended up having five handbell groups, and they played very often in church worship services.

Now you can take "Handbells 101" in college and graduate school—and what a wonderful experience for the young music minister. College students can really do remarkable things with handbells under disciplined leadership. Adults can do remarkable things with handbells under disciplined leadership!

If you aren't familiar with handbells, books are available that detail everything you have always wanted to know about handbells. There are videocassette tapes for study. Seminars, clinics, and festivals are offered where you can learn the basics of handbell ringing. And you can probably visit a church not far from yours that has a full handbell program, enabling you to learn from them.

Handbells are worth the effort! They are good therapy for the ringers and for the conductor.

INSTRUMENTALISTS can bring both joy and excitement to a worship experience/major performance . . . and INSTRUMENTALISTS can make you very frustrated. But preparation is the key to working with INSTRUMENTALISTS. If you know where you are going, what you are doing, what to expect of them, provide them marked scores, and give full and complete instructions, you will get along just fine in the rehearsal and performance.

One final word: In dealing with INSTRUMENTALISTS, don't waste time—for time is money! You'll learn this very quickly. Remember to move the rehearsal along, and don't get bogged down in rehearsal that doesn't affect the INSTRUMENTALISTS!

In the heavenly orchestra, I want to play French horn!

J
Janitor

"He who has clean hands . . ." (Ps. 24:4).

One of the unsung heros of any local church congregation is the janitor/custodian/maintenance person. He does a lot of hard work sweeping, cleaning, polishing, setting up chairs and tables, taking down chairs and tables, is bossed by every member of the church family, and rarely, if ever, gets any commendation from anyone!

The music ministry uses the JANITOR as much as anyone, especially if rooms have to be set up weekly for graded choirs, handbells, choir rehearsal, instrumental rehearsal, and the like.

The relationship between JANITOR and music minister should be a good one, positive and happy. If not, one may find cleanliness a consistent source of frustration.

So it becomes a pleasure to make sure the JANITOR is appreciated often for the extra things that are done in the music area . . . and beyond.

Have a JANITOR Appreciation Night following choir rehearsal one week, and let the choir thank the person for keeping the facility clean for them. Have cake, punch, and all the party favors in his honor. Decorate the room with janitorial supplies!

Janitor

Certainly, on a regular basis say a simple thank you to your maintenance staff. Go out of your way to express your appreciation to them in person, with thank-you notes, and by treating them in a positive manner.

Make sure your needs are made known well in advance, so the JANITOR can see to them in his own time. It is very unfair and frustrating to him for you to run in and demand that a room be set up in ten minutes so you can have a rehearsal. Perhaps weekly, in staff meetings, needs of the ministerial staff can be outlined and given to the maintenance staff in writing.

If your relationship with the JANITOR is not good, it may be wise for you to communicate and work through his staff supervisor, giving him your needs and requirements and letting the supervisor pass along these needs. But it is best for you to do it yourself, if at all possible . . . and if this is the proper procedure. Some churches desire that all maintenance needs go through the minister of education or another staff member responsible for this area.

Encourage the people to whom you are responsible to also be appreciative to the maintenance staff. We are prone many times to jump on somebody for missing an assignment, but we are often remiss in not expressing a simple thank you for consistent good work and clean facilities. So . . . to the JANITOR . . . here is a big . . .

Thank You!

K
Keyboardists

"Praise him with stringed instruments and organ" (Ps. 150:4, KJV).

Blessed is the individual who has good KEYBOARDISTS, for when he makes an error, they will cover for him.

Blessed is the individual who has good KEYBOARDISTS, for they will make him look very good.

Blessed is the individual who has good KEYBOARDISTS, for they giveth good support to the choral and congregational sound.

Blessed is the individual who has good KEYBOARDISTS, for when he asks for quiet support, they give him quiet support.

Yes, the music minister who has people at the organ and piano who are sharp, committed musicians, supportive of the total program, willing to adjust and be flexible, and willing to play all kinds of music . . . is truly blessed. There are very few things as hard on a minister of music as an accompanist who "fights" the music minister . . . who won't play "Amazing Grace" . . . who always plays too loud . . . who won't take instruction or follow directions . . . who wants to be "director from the keyboard" . . . who is in competition with the director . . . who makes snide remarks about the director . . . who sight-reads through an important rehearsal . . . and so on!

KEYBOARDISTS are generally wonderful, committed people who love the Lord, who enjoy playing, accompanying, and supporting the music ministry and the total church program. There are some things that the music minister can do to help relations with the KEYBOARDISTS and seal the bond of ministry between the two (or three) of them.

• Never embarrass the KEYBOARDIST . . . in public or in private. This is a good way to commit "musical suicide"! If there is a problem, visit with the KEYBOARDIST privately but never air your displeasure in public, especially not in front of the choir.

• Rehearse with the KEYBOARDISTS in advance when there are specific places you wish to change or alter. Call attention to specifics in this private rehearsal and not in front of the choir.

• Do not expect your KEYBOARDISTS to sight-read difficult material on the spot. Do not pull out a new, difficult anthem and ask the choir to read through it if the KEYBOARDISTS have not seen it prior to this rehearsal. This is in poor taste and shows a lack of concern and regard for the person at the keyboard.

• Give the KEYBOARDISTS the choir music for as many weeks in advance as you can. A good rule of thumb to follow is: Prepare your music schedule from January through May, June through August, and September through December. You then have three "semesters" to organize your music, get things on paper, and distribute instructions to the KEYBOARDISTS and the choir.

Set up the Sundays of each month and select your anthems accordingly, using the seasons and special holidays as a guide. Order any new music ahead of time and give your KEYBOARDISTS a list of the anthems, the numbers, and the Sunday when they will be sung. This schedule makes the music minister plan ahead—and this is a good thing! There are some music ministers who finish a rehearsal on Wednesday evening and, following the rehearsal, do not know which anthem the choir will sing on Sunday! This is poor management of time and energy and very frustrating to your KEYBOARDISTS and the choir!

Of course, the prepared schedule may change when necessary. You may add or drop a particular anthem from the schedule, but the majority of the pieces will stay intact. And you have something from which to work.

* Know what to expect of your KEYBOARDISTS; know their strengths and their weaknesses. It is useless to give a piece of music to an accompanist when you know in your heart that even when he practices and practices and practices, he won't be able to play it correctly.

For instance, some of the rhythmically difficult contemporary pieces take a real gift or "feel" for rhythm. Some KEYBOARDISTS will never attain that "feel" to bring it off. It will be very labored and everyone will know it, especially you.

Choose your choral literature carefully, and keep it within the boundaries of the skill of your KEYBOARDISTS. Challenge them but do not discourage or frustrate them! Make them stretch and grow. Give them literature that will make them want to work and prepare carefully.

* The KEYBOARDISTS should be given a copy of the morning and evening worship plans prior to Sunday morning when they arrive at the church!

Again, this is advance planning—careful planning. Services can be planned for a month at a time, with copies given to the KEYBOARDISTS at the beginning of each month. They can see what hymns will be sung, what "free accompaniments" can be used, and what anthems, responses, and other service music will be used.

The Lord admonishes us to do things "decently and in order," and this certainly should apply to the order of worship and the celebration in the worship experience. Too often we leave the service planning until the last minute and then wonder why our worship services lack creativity, planning, excitement!

There should never be "holes" in the worship service program! This means there should never be a listing for "hymn" and no number—no title. There should never be a listing for "special music" with no title/composer. There should never be a listing for "soloist" with no song title, composer/arranger, and soloist. There should never be a listing for "offertory," "prelude," or "postlude" without a title and composer/arranger.

All of this takes advance work, careful planning, and being on the ball to make sure everything is in order and in the order of worship.

- Compliment your KEYBOARDISTS often, in private and in public. These are important people who do excellent work—and for the most part, with little or no pay for their services. Celebrate their birthdays in choir rehearsal. Celebrate special events with them. Include them in worship planning. Make them feel a part of the staff by including them in staff meeting at least once a month. Ask their opinion often. Anything you can do to increase their respect of you as music minister will be to your advantage in the long run. A good working relationship with the KEYBOARDISTS is essential for a successful program.

KEYBOARDISTS are certainly essential to the making of music. A good working relationship between the

KEYBOARDISTS and the music minister is absolutely necessary and desired.

So . . . long live the keyboard . . . and those who play it! May your tribe increase and your abilities increase along with your tribe!

L
Laymen

". . . be all the more diligent to make certain about His calling and choosing you" (2 Pet. 1:10).

Some of God's choicest servants throughout history have been LAYMEN (the term *laywomen* is synonymous here with LAYMEN). You know the stories of those wonderful Bible characters who were not ministers, but served God faithfully while they worked in the marketplace of life.

There are many contemporary LAYMEN who also serve God and work in the marketplace of life. Everyone who reads this book will picture a flood of LAYMEN who were faithful to God, responsible to the local church, honest in their dealings, a force for good in their community, and vitally concerned for the kingdom of God.

Five dollars was a lot of money back in 1958 when my wife, Esther, and I were first married. We served the First Baptist Church, Lindsey, Oklahoma, while we were students at Oklahoma Baptist University. T. J. Goodner, one of God's choicest servants in that Oklahoma community, owned the local food store. Weekly, as Esther and I shopped for the weekend groceries, T. J. would shake one of our hands and leave five dollars in it, saying, "God bless you both!"

Every Saturday night Esther and I would go to the home of "Aunt Maud" for dinner and to watch "Gunsmoke" on her little TV. She insisted that we young marrieds come over and eat with her and get at least one good meal per weekend!

The Larry Beards, First Baptist Church, Muskogee, Oklahoma, would have Esther and me over for Christmas Eve dinner every year we served that church, to let us be part of their larger family since we could not get to our family at Christmas. They became family to us. And the Troy Bakers had us for Christmas brunch every year, just because they loved us and wanted to share their Christmas morning with the music minister and his wife.

And there was James Day, Calvary Baptist Church, Denison, Texas, who loved this young music minister and his wife. I was attending Southwestern Seminary and commuted back and forth between Denison and Fort Worth twice each week. Esther stayed in Denison because she was expecting our first child. Something happened and she lost that first baby. Heartbroken and saddened, we returned home from the hospital. James didn't know what to say or do. He struggled with us in our sorrow. Every day he would come by our little apartment after working all day at the Pillsbury factory. He would bring an ice cream cone in his hand, dripping down his sleeve, and would say to Esther: "I'll keep coming and bringing you ice cream cones till I see the light return to your eyes." And he did just that. He brought the love of God to her, wrapped up in an ice cream cone.

Faye and Mack Brown, First Baptist Church, Abilene, Texas, along with their two daughters, one son, two dogs, and five pigs, took us in. They became our "extended family," helping us in the birth of our son, raising our daughter, showing them (and us) the value of sharing your family with others—something we have tried to do ever since that exposure to the Browns.

The Jarrell Estes family, Birmingham, Alabama, literally raised our daughter, Melody, during those difficult junior high-senior high years when she didn't care for us. Jarrell and Sarah had three daughters of their own, so one more didn't make any difference to them! These LAYMEN ministered to us in some very special ways outside the church building. And that seems to me to have been exactly what Christ did during His days on earth. He ministered outside the church building to the needs of people.

Each of you also knows some key people who have affected your lives who were LAYMEN! Thank God for LAYMEN!

But there are also LAYMEN who feel it is God's calling in their lives to keep the staff and church family humble. Some of these think they have been called to be negative on every issue, to fight every proposal, and to be unmovable on important issues that affect the life of a church. And these are both old and young men/women! Age doesn't seem to be a factor here—vision is! But you can learn from these LAYMEN too! They can teach you valuable lessons about human nature and how to minister to all kinds of people in the ministry to which you have been called.

I believe in LAYMEN—and I believe that LAYMEN hold the key to the success or failure of the local church. The staff can take the local church only as far as the congregation will let them. Supportive, influential LAYMEN have helped many churches go beyond themselves and do the impossible because of their faith in God, their belief in their ministerial staff, and their support of the total church program, built on the will of God in the life of that church.

I thank the LAYMEN who serve faithfully in the local church, who love the Father, who give of their valuable time to serve on committees that make the hard decisions, who get little or no thanks for any of the work done, but who get lots of flak when things don't go right! God has depended on LAYMEN throughout history and will continue to do so till He chooses to come again and reclaim His own people.

And . . . special thanks to the Goodners, "Aunt Maud," the Beards, the Bakers, the Days, the Browns, and the Esteses! And the many, many other wonderful LAYMEN who have impacted the lives of Bob and Esther Burroughs!

M
Motivation

". . . to encourage them in the work of the house of God . . ." (Ezra 6:22).

The ability to motivate people is a rare gift indeed. MOTIVATION is a golden key to success in any church program, especially in the ministry of music.

MOTIVATION is that special something that flows into the rehearsal, the worship experience, the committee meeting that gives people insight and excitement and leaves them with positive feelings when it is over.

There should be a class in graduate school that teaches young people the skill of MOTIVATION. This skill does not come easily. But rather than begging, cajoling, and pleading with people to do a task, to be at a rehearsal, or to serve on a committee, how much better it would be to have people anxious to do these things. This is the result of good MOTIVATION by staff or other leaders.

So how does one go about motivating someone to do something? Here are some suggestions from years of experience:

- Be positive in your approach. Instead of lamenting that fourteen persons were absent from the choir rehearsal this week, promote the fact that thirty-four persons were present! Don't lambast the youth choir because exams caused twenty-four to stay away from rehearsal and study; celebrate the fact that sixteen did show up and you accomplished something—even though you may have to reteach the same thing next week!

We who minister seem to always be on the lookout for the "one lost sheep" and forget to tend the ninety-nine who are faithful, active, and ready to go. We worry about the fourteen absent and want to write them letters to encourage them to return next week—and this should be done! But we should certainly celebrate in the number present. Once in a while we should write them a letter thanking them for their faithfulness—or phone them to say thank you for being present last rehearsal. Being concerned about the "one lost sheep" so often may cause some of the ninety-nine to lose interest; and you may be looking for more "lost sheep" than you would care to try to find!

• Be professional in your ministry—to the point that the people know when they come to a rehearsal, a committee meeting, a worship service, a banquet, or whatever, it will be done in a first-class, orderly manner, with little or no time wasted. Laypeople are busy too—with their own lives, jobs, family, and outside activities. To come to a rehearsal or committee meeting where precious time is lost (a) waiting on the latecomers, (b) still preparing for the meeting when it should have already begun, (c) gossiping and wasting good energy frustrates laypeople. They lose any MOTIVATION they might have had for the position and their sense of responsibility wanes.

• Be up to date with your plans, and project dates in advance for your people. Many ministers live "by the week," and anything that happens two weeks from now is not even under consideration! Your calendars need to be full of plans for the coming month, six months, year, five years!

People in advertising tell us that it takes eleven exposures to something before it begins to register with the average consumer. If we translate this into church work, it takes eleven contacts, announcements, or bulletin inserts to make people aware of a dinner, rehearsal, performance, special guest, or tithing day, and it will not do to have it in the announcement sheet once or twice. People will not be aware—and they will not respond! This is especially true in the metropolitan areas of this country. There is far too much to do with their valuable time. When the church *expects* people to be there with little or no warning time, the church is courting disaster.

Give your people a calendar of projected activities for the coming year. Then give committees one for the coming six months and three months. Highlight for your choirs the events for which they will be responsible. Put these dates/times down for them to see often—and regularly. Comment often about an upcoming event. Continually make them aware—and even then some will still forget or get the date mixed up.

The minister who does not plan in advance does not have good motivational skills. It is as simple as that. If you are one who is not a detail person, who does not look to the future and does not do advance planning, your program suffers from this lack of personal discipline.

• There is a difference in being a motivator and a cheerleader. Cheerleaders we do not need. Motivators we do need. Cheerleaders "hype" for the moment—they take care of the present and lead people right now. Motivators are consistent, disciplined people who keep their people informed, aware, conscious, and excited for the duration of the project.

- MOTIVATION is a learned skill. It is not a "gift of the Spirit." One learns to motivate carefully and gently. One learns to motivate by failing and succeeding and evaluating the two, deciding what caused the failure and the success. MOTIVATION skills grow slowly, as you are exposed to success and failure.

Every staff member needs to be a motivator, especially the ministerial staff. If a program is failing, it is probably due to the lack of MOTIVATION from the staff to the people and from the people to the staff.

You can learn to motivate! It will increase your ministry possibilities. It will make you more professional in your assignments. It will give you success in your programs. MOTIVATION—a valuable key to success.

N
New vs. Old

". . . old things are passed away; behold, new things have come" (2 Cor. 5:17).

"Let's sing the OLD hymns!" "Why don't you ever do anything NEW?" "I like the OLD songs." "NEW hymns speak to our society." "If it ain't OLD, I won't sing it!" "Thanks for teaching us a NEW hymn." "I don't like the NEW hymnal! It's too heavy!"

If there is a bigger controversy in any church than NEW vs. OLD, it must be some controversy! People ask me often: "What's NEW?" No one has ever asked, "What's good?" And some of the NEW is not good—and much of the OLD is neither good nor up to date.

The Bible speaks loudly and clearly about the NEW and the OLD:

- Psalm 33:3: "Sing to [the Lord] a NEW song."
- Ecclesiastes 1:9: ". . . nothing NEW under the sun."
- Ezekiel 11:19: ". . . put a NEW spirit within them."
- John 13:34: "A NEW commandment I give to you."
- Ephesians 4:24: "Put on the NEW self . . ."
- 2 Corinthians 5:17: ". . . OLD things are passed away."
- Colossians 3:9: ". . . laid aside the OLD self . . ."

We live in the twentieth century, and many of you will live to see the dawn of the twenty-first century. We are living in a society in which nothing is of less value than yesterday's newspaper! Yet in church work we tend to live in the past, especially with our hymnology. We sing of another era, another time, the "good old days," the old-time religion.

There is value in feeling comfortable and "at home" in the church, and there is security in singing what we know. But sometimes in singing what we know, we do not know what we are singing.

Here are two lines from one of the most popular hymns in the United States: "Trim your feeble lamps, my brother. Let the lower lights be burning." Now let me ask you three questions: (1) What are "feeble lamps"? (2) How do you trim them? (3) What are "lower lights"?

Obviously, this hymn was written in another age, before electricity! The answers: (1) "Feeble lamps" are kerosene lanterns that have wicks, and when the flame burns low, (2) the wick must be "trimmed," or raised so the flame can reach it. (3) "Lower lights" were the lights along the shore, leading up to the big lighthouse, warning ships of dangerous waters.

You see, this hymn, though popular, is obviously out of date. Yet our congregations sing it anyway, never even bothering to explain the text to a generation that has grown up in the age of electricity—where "feeble lamps" are not even in the vocabulary!

"Alas, and did my Saviour bleed? And did my Sovereign die? Would He devote that sacred head For such a worm as I?" Another very familiar hymn . . . but the terminology is dated. We do not call people "worms" these days in conversation. This has been changed to "sinners such as I" in newer hymnals, making the hymn contemporary in language and meaning.

Some hymns seem to be ageless. They are as profound today as three hundred years ago. "A Mighty

Fortress," "Praise, My Soul, The King of Heaven," "Joyful, Joyful, We Adore Thee"—all are still contemporary in thought. Why? The great hymns that last from generation to generation seem to be the hymns that speak of the majesty and power of God. The hymns that are dated rather quickly seem to be hymns that deal with other subjects, such as self. Many of the hymns with "I" in them seem to date themselves quickly.

There is pressure on the worship leaders to plan the worship services with the OLD hymns predominant in the service. But any minister who is truly trying to minister to his total congregation will give priority to the delicate balance of NEW vs. OLD. Churches and church programs do not grow when they throw out everything that is NEW and provide only the OLD.

Where we lose balance is not providing enough exposure to the NEW, while yielding to the pressure to do the OLD. Let's face it—some of the OLD is out of date and not at all relevant to the present church, her people, and her ministry. Yet we struggle on, singing these dated hymns and not even bothering to explain them to the young people.

It seems that the music minister should be "middle of the road" when it comes to music selection. This includes hymns and anthems. Certainly, no one can please every member of every church every Sunday in worship. Someone will not like a hymn or the anthem or the postlude (if anyone listens to the postlude). But the music minister who has a minister's heart will seek to give enough variety in the service to please the vast majority of the congregation week by week.

If you sing a NEW anthem this Sunday, provide the congregation with a couple of OLD hymns to balance the service. If you sing a standard "sugar stick" anthem, feel free to include in the order of worship a NEW or relatively unfamiliar hymn.

While we are discussing the NEW vs. OLD, let us talk a few moments about anthems, since this book is primarily intended for music ministers.

Anthems are like hymns. Some tend to be able to live from generation to generation and still be fresh and vibrant. Others quickly fall by the wayside and are good for nothing but to collect dust in the library.

Too many church musicians seek the "next big hit" like a heat-seeking missile! Some musicians go from big musical production to big musical production, using the latest tunes, texts, lights, cameras, and action. "What's new?" is their watchword! If it's new, let's do it! So we buy the latest musical and force feed our choirs more of what was successful the last time!

Many music ministers are forcing their own musical values and tastes on their church people. Everyone in your choir does not like Bach just because you like Bach. And if you *love* Gaither, not everyone in your choir will like a steady dose of Gaither!

Be flexible. Loosen up a bit! Give your people a wide variety of materials so that at least once per month, almost everyone can say they worshiped because of the music.

Just because an anthem has a 1957 copyright date on it does not mean it is dated material. "Awake, My Heart" by Jane Marshall (H. W. Gray) has a 1957 copyright, and it is still a classic and should be sung today. "Follow Me" by Roger Wilson (Lorenz) has a 1942 copyright date on it—but it has a Longfellow text that is current and will be meaningful to your people. There are many anthems with this year's copyright year on them that are already dated!

Be careful in your selection of music. Look carefully

at texts to see what they are saying to your people. Look at some older pieces as well as the new things. Look for variety of style, feeling, flow, text, musicianship, structure. Allow your people the freedom to enjoy other literature, even if you do not enjoy it as much as Bach.

Here is a gift for you! Listed below are twenty-five "oldies-but-goodies" that are still relative to today's market, still selling well, and as contemporary as today's paper. I know you'll thank me, so I'll just say it now: "You're welcome." Any one of these anthems will be enjoyed by your choir—I guarantee each one. They have been tested by fire and found worthy of your consideration. They are listed alphabetically.

1. "Alleluia," John Zaumeyer, SATB, A Cappella, © 1960 (Warner Brothers—W3669)

2. "Ascription of Praise," David Schwoebel, SATB, Piano, © 1983 (Hinshaw Music, HMC-615)

3. "Build Thee More Stately Mansions," Gordon Young, SATB, Organ, © 1959 (Presser—312-40405)

4. "Cast Thy Burden upon the Lord," Claude L. Bass, SATB, Piano, © 1961 (Genevox—4561-07)

5. "For the Beauty of the Earth," John Rutter, SATB, Piano, © 1980 (Hinshaw—HMC-550)

6. "Jesus, My Lord, My Life, My All," Bob Burroughs, SATB, A Cappella, © 1963 (Tempo—KS1232B)

7. "Jesus, Thou Joy of Loving Hearts," Claude L. Bass, SATB, Piano, © 1960 (Genevox—4535-39)

8. "I Will Not Leave You Comfortless," Everett Titcomb, SATB, A Cappella, © 1964 (Carl Fischer—CM441)

9. "Let Your Joy Be Known," Fred Bock, SATB, Organ, © 1969 (Word—3010005164)

10. "Love," Bob Burroughs, SATB, Piano, © 1976 (Sonshine Productions—SP101)

New vs. Old

11. "More Love to Thee," Bob Burroughs, SATB, Piano, Flute, © 1975 (Genevox—4562-50)

12. "Now Sing We Joyfully unto God," Gordon Young, SATB, Organ, © 1962 (Shawnee Press—A-651)

13. "O Come, Let Us Sing to the Lord," Louis Harris, SATB, Organ, Two Optional Trumpets, © 1978 (Word—301-0003015)

14. "O My Soul, What Love," Lanny Allen, SATB, Piano, © 1975 (Word—301-0002713)

15. "Praise God!" Fred Bock, SATB, Organ, © 1971 (Sacred Music Press—S-113)

16. "Praise the Lord, Our God, Forever," Mozart, Arr. Ehret, SATB, Piano, © 1980 (Fred Bock Music Company—B-G0176)

17. "Praise Ye the Lord," David H. Williams, SATB, Piano, © 1959 (Fred Bock Music Company—B-G0524)

18. "Prayer Before Singing," Don Hustad, SATB, A Cappella, © 1959 (Hope Music—HA-107)

19. "Psalm 86," Carl Nygard, SATB, Piano, © 1984 (Hinshaw Music—HMC-755)

20. "Song of Exaltation," John Ness Beck, SATB, Piano, © 1967 (G. Schirmer—46267)

21. "Surely, He Has Borne Our Griefs," John Carter, SATB, Piano, © 1977 (Beckenhorst—BP1042)

22. "The Lord Is My Shepherd," Thomas Matthews, SATB, Organ, © 1956 (H. T. Fitzsmmons—F2137)

23. "The Majesty and Glory of Your Name," Tom Fettke and Linda Johnson, SATB, Piano, © 1979 (Word Music—302-0002954)

24. "The Lord Is My Shepherd," John Carter, Two-Part, Piano, © 1984 (Hope—A555)

25. "When I Survey the Wondrous Cross," Arr. Gilbert M. Martin, SATB, Organ, © 1970 (Presser—312-40785)

O
Officers

"It is a trustworthy statement: if any man aspires to the office of overseer, it is a fine work he desires to do" (1 Tim. 3:1).

Choir OFFICERS are either overworked and undercomplimented, or they are ignored and have little or no responsibilities. There doesn't seem to be much middle ground.

Music ministers cannot do everything by themselves, even though many have literally died trying. OFFICERS can be a godsend for music ministers, if the ministers will allow them room to assist and grow in the position.

First of all, some general observations about OFFICERS:

- There are usually far too many OFFICERS for the size of the choir.
- Visit with prospective OFFICERS in advance of their being elected to see whether, if elected, they will be willing to serve the choir in the position they are being offered. If they "hem and haw" around, thank them for their consideration and look elsewhere for someone who will work if elected! Do not strap yourself and the choir with OFFICERS who are halfhearted in

their feelings about the office and the responsibility they would carry.

- OFFICERS lose interest in their position when it is longer than six months. Choirs that elect OFFICERS for one year usually get only six months of work out of those people, and the program suffers. There is an excitement among OFFICERS about a schedule that runs from January through June and July through December because the OFFICERS do not have a full year to worry about. They can get on with their lives the remainder of the time. I would never again elect choir OFFICERS for longer than six months! Try it and you will never go back to the old way of one-year terms! (Sounds like prison, doesn't it?)

- A regular OFFICERS meeting at least once per month is vital. This is time well spent, even if it is following Wednesday night choir rehearsal and everyone is dead tired, including the director. It is still important to allow the OFFICERS time to do their thing, which will eventually help the music minister! At this meeting, projected plans (banquets, birthdays, concerts, etc.) should be outlined and discussed in detail. Problems should be aired. Choir members will feel free to discuss problems with OFFICERS who will not tell the music minister who gave the information. OFFICERS can be a good sounding board for potential problems and solutions. Compliments need to be given. Make the OFFICERS meeting a good "family time," and compliment each OFFICER in person, in front of the other OFFICERS. Let them know they are appreciated.

- Make sure every OFFICER is busy. Be sure he/she has something to do regularly. Nothing is more boring than to be an OFFICER with nothing to do. Prepare an OFFICERS' duty sheet, and make sure each OFFICER has one at the beginning of the term of office . . . and understands the ramifications of the job. Walk each

OFFICER through the job after he or she has been elected. Check on the OFFICERS regularly and see that they are contacting people, writing letters, making phone calls, filing music, working with robes, collecting money, or whatever they are supposed to do!

• Let the OFFICERS be seen by the choir as they do their jobs. Let them have their say in rehearsals. Let the people know that these positions are valuable and there is a responsibility to being a choir OFFICER.

• Keep your very best people involved in the ministry of being a choir OFFICER. Do not give a position to someone as an honor! People should be elected to be an OFFICER the "old-fashioned way—they earn it!"

• Do not give music minister responsibilities to OFFICERS! You are the music minister—not them; and they should not be doing your visitation, your correspondence, your dirty work.

• Discuss the issue with a choir OFFICER when he or she fails to carry out the job. If an OFFICER isn't carrying out assigned responsibilities, visit with the person privately and see if there is a problem of which you are not aware. Sickness at home may keep your social chairman from providing snacks or cleaning up the mess. Find out why and deal with it. They will respect you for asking and will consider it ministry because you care enough to check up on them.

The number of OFFICERS and their responsibilities will vary depending upon the size of the church, the size of the choir, and the concepts of the music minister. I think most choirs have too many OFFICERS. There are sometimes more OFFICERS than members or prospects. The fewer the better is a good motto. Establish a policy that allows you just enough OFFICERS to get the job done and keep the organization running smoothly and efficiently. That's all you need to make choir work!

Officers

The following OFFICER list has worked for me through the years. Try it on for size.

The *president* is the key to a successful choir program. His/her faithfulness, attitude, humor, and responsibility to this office should be evident to the other choir members. He/she should be well liked by the other people. This person, in reality, is the assistant to the music minister and is in the "people business." He/she should know his/her people, prospects, visitors, and be able to assist with robes, folders, seating— the works.

Allow the president to either open or close the rehearsal with announcements and comments and to handle those details that the music minister usually does after finishing a hard rehearsal. The president should check with the music minister prior to rehearsal to make sure there is a list of things to go over in rehearsal—and this puts some responsibility back on the music minister to make sure something is happening!

The president checks with the other OFFICERS regularly to see if things are going smoothly and to see if assistance is needed to fulfill the job.

The president is the "go-between" for the choir and the music minister. He needs to keep his "ear to the people," so to speak, and let the music minister know of potential problems with music, rehearsals, or people.

The president should be a motivator of people, encouraging and gently nudging them along to be better than they are.

The president should be the sounding board for the music minister—someone on whom he can rely on for advice, counsel, and straight talk. They should be good friends, full of trust for each other.

Choir should be a priority event for the choir president. One cannot do a good job serving the choir and be responsible for five other things in the church—and do any of them well.

The *social vice-president* is responsible for seeing that the choir rehearsal is a happy time! Happiness comes in a variety of ways to a variety of people, and many different and exciting options are open to the social VP. Weekly refreshments are always welcome. Coffee, ice, soft drinks, cookies, light cake, and dips are easy to fix and relatively inexpensive. The social VP should work through the social committee to see that no one person—or section—carries major responsibility. The social committee may consist of as many people as the social VP desires to have on the committee. Some people prefer to work alone. Others prefer to work with the masses. Whichever way the social VP chooses is best for him/her!

The refreshment table probably should be set up outside the choir rehearsal facility, unless you are fortunate to have a large rehearsal room with plenty of space. Lots of fellowship goes on around this table, and it should be in a place where it will not interfere with the beginning or middle of rehearsal. There can be refreshments every rehearsal or on special occasions. "Surprises" can be fun things—under the chair, in the chair, over the chair—but not often enough for the members to expect something! Surprises are fun unless they are expected. The choir suite should be decorated often. Decorations should be simple. Decorations should be done at a time other than rehearsal.

Surprises, decorations, refreshments—all need to be cleaned up at the appropriate time, so the choir doesn't come in the room the next time and find remnants of last week's rehearsal on the chairs, walls, or floor!

If the social committee decorates for a season (such as spring), these decorations can stay up longer. But if

Officers

they decorate for an event (such as Valentine's Day) decorations should come down soon after the rehearsal.

Make choir fun, exciting, interesting, and the talk of the town. Or at least the talk of the church! That's one way to get people interested in your program—excitement.

Do all things decently and in good order—in advance, neat, and clean.

Any needs of the social VP should be made known to the president. Large trash cans would be nice, as would a regular supply of coffee, artificial sweetener, sugar, napkins, cups, and other necessary items. Someone needs to have the responsibility of seeing that these items are on the table and ready. And someone needs to be ready to clean up too!

Choir parties, banquets, and surprises should be items high on your list. When should you have such events? It is difficult to say; with the crowded schedules that people have these days, every church choir must set its own agenda. Too much activity will surely fail. Yet too little does not make a "choir family."

Within a year, the following suggestions might be open to discussion by the OFFICERS and the choir:

January: "New Choir Year" Party—first rehearsal

February: Valentine Party or Banquet; perhaps an after-choir snack supper with small sandwiches, etc.

March: St. Patrick's Day—everyone required to attend rehearsal in green—and those who show up without green will be given something green to wear as they enter the room! Green refreshments and punch; "Welcome to Spring" Party

April: April Fools—obviously! Have a "backwards" choir rehearsal where the room is completely backwards; have April Fools surprises

May: End-of-School-Party; End-of-Choir-Year Banquet—at church or in someone's *large* home

June: Welcome to Summer

July: July Fourth

August: End-of-Summer Banquet; Composer's Weekend, with Banquet; Music Ministry Banquet

September: Back-to-School Party; Back-to-Choir Party—Enlistment Time

October: Welcome to Fall

November: Thanksgiving Banquet; Thanksgiving Snack Time; Winter Wonderland

December: Christmas

These are just sketchy ideas to get the creative juices flowing. Go from here and create fun things and surprises. Make the choir room, the people, the robe rooms come alive with fun, food, fellowship, and good feelings about each other and the church!

The *membership vice-president* should know the people well! This person and the committee is responsible for three major things:

- maintaining good choir attendance—consistently
- finding ways to help the choir grow
- maintaining good choir attendance—consistently

So let's take them one at a time:

1. The membership VP and a committee (if needed) should call those who are absent two times in a row, either on Sundays or rehearsal nights. Find out what is going on and how the choir can be of service or help. Inform the music minister and president if problems exist.

Do not keep persons on the choir rolls forever just because they have always been members! Come up with a good plan to keep the membership current. Come up with a way to "refresh the rolls" every six months. This will mean, of course, reassigning robes, books, etc.; but if it will keep people current, it will be worth it!

2. How can you keep the choir growing? How can

Officers

you reach out into the community and appeal to people with the choir, the music ministry of our church? Are there people who have sung in this choir before who might be interested in singing again? How can you enlist new people from the community who need to be singing? Discuss these questions and others with the officers—regularly, consistently. Keep on the lookout for new people. Choir members will "come out of the woodwork" to be involved in an active, exciting, innovative, and consistently rewarding music ministry. It has been proven over and over again.

3. When visitors or new members attend choir rehearsal, they should be met by the membership VP, taken to their section (be sure and ask them what they sing), given a folder, and shown where it belongs when they are through with it. Introduce them to someone in the section who will look after them during the rehearsal and explain how the "system" works. If they desire to come on Sunday morning and sing, make sure they will have a robe, folder, hymnal, and anything else they need. See that they are being introduced and welcomed, and make sure people are getting involved in the "helping" process.

The key ingredient here is making the prospect feel at home, comfortable, welcome. Many times a prospect will come to choir and be literally ignored by everyone—not on purpose, but because everyone is happy to be at rehearsal, happy to have a cup of fresh coffee, happy to see friends, happy to be getting ready to sing again. They forget about being a one-person welcoming committee when someone new arrives on the scene. But they can be trained over a period of time, and a warm welcome will work wonders for your visitors! They will feel included in your choir family almost immediately and will desire to come back for more.

The *secretary* should keep accurate records of the

choir, making the music minister, president, and membership VP aware of people who have been out more than twice in a row. During the rehearsal, the secretary should check the attendance. He or she may know the choir well enough to tell who is present or absent by looking around at each section. The secretary will fill out the absentee slip and see that the membership VP and music minister get one following rehearsal. The list can be used to do lots of things! Then the membership VP can call each absentee following rehearsal. The choir can be given postcards and each member can write one or more of these people a postcard on the spot. If you have a weekly choir paper, each absentee should be sent a choir paper the next morning, to allow them to keep up with the choir news. The membership VP can assign certain people to call a certain absentee during the week.

The secretary should work up a monthly or quarterly list of attendance averages, by sections and overall percentage of both rehearsals and performances. Note those with 100 percent attendance in both performance and rehearsal, those with 100 percent attendance in rehearsal or performance, and other accomplishments. Publish these in the choir paper.

The *treasurer*, as might be expected, is responsible for handling the money of the choir. A monthly report should be given to the president, explaining receipts and expenditures. This can be published in the choir paper. The choir fund becomes the responsibility of the treasurer. The "25-cent-per-week" per member idea is worth consideration. You might recommend that each choir member consider giving 25 cents per week, one dollar per month, or twelve dollars per year to support the choir ministry. The basket should be passed weekly, giving the choir members an opportunity to be a part of sending flowers to the choir members and/or immediate family who might be ill, sending birthday cards to choir members, or helping pay for the refreshments. The treasurer should be creative in the passing of the hat. Pass a box or a cute basket. The more clever the gimmick, the more money will be collected.

The music budget should be responsible for the music ministry, but the choir fund does the small, intimate things for the choir family.

In smaller choirs the positions of secretary and treasurer might be combined into one position. In larger choirs a secretary for each section, responsible to the main secretary, might be a good idea.

The *robe/folder chairperson* is responsible for seeing that every person on roll has a robe that fits (somewhat), a folder, and a hymnal to call his/her own! Nothing is more frustrating than not to have your own robe or folder on a consistent basis—and to have to stand around until everyone is in place and select what is left. Let the membership VP know what robes/folders are available on a regular basis. Keep the robes in good condition. They should be cleaned every four to six months, depending upon a lot of things, including how hot the choir loft is in summer, how much perspiring the people do, how often the robes are dropped on the floor, etc.

The *librarian* is responsible for:
- keeping the choir music library in good shape, clean and neat;
- keeping choir folders clean of bulletins, tissue, candy, and other items too strange to mention here;
- taking music out of the folders that has been sung on recent Sundays. This should be done about every three weeks;
- putting new music in the folders;
- cataloging new music in a filing system that is easy to understand and easy to use;

- making sure the number of copies is up to date with the number of people in the choir. If "Create in Me a Clean Heart" by Carl Mueller is to be sung soon and there are only twenty-four copies for your sixty-voice choir, someone has dropped the ball.

The librarian should always check the anthems listed for spring, summer, fall, or winter against the number of copies in the library and see that ample copies are ordered. Choir members do not like to share music!

That is about it for choir OFFICERS. But, you say, what about *section leaders* and a host of other officer positions? The answer is simple: If you need them, elect them. If you won't use them, don't bother with them. Section leaders may be all right for the large megachoirs; but for any choir under about fifty persons, there are few conductors who need section leaders to do musical work with their choirs. So all a section leader really does is become a mini-secretary to that section. It is true that the officers mentioned in this section will have to work a bit harder, for the responsibilities are greater and the number of people are fewer. But the term of office is only six months—and the OFFICERS will give their best because they don't have to do the job for one year!

There is no place in this book to talk about choir constitutions and all those formal things. The choir constitutions that have come across my desk have all been full of technicalities and what ifs. I find little real value to a choir constitution. I believe that choir is choir . . . and choir is family . . . and choir is using this avenue of responsibility to serve the Father . . . and choir is loving each other and caring for each other . . . and choir is making sure everyone absent is contacted regularly . . . and choir is making sure the OFFICERS do their jobs . . . and choir is the OFFICERS taking care of the choir family . . . and choir is doing the best job we can Sunday after Sunday, in praise of Christ, the King.

Support those OFFICERS—and they will support you.

P
Pastor/Staff

"Now there are varieties of gifts, but the same Spirit. And there are varieties of ministries, but the same Lord" (1 Cor. 12:4-5).

PASTOR/STAFF—happy times, grand adventures in the faith, the thrill of leading a congregation further into personal commitment with Christ, the joys of sharing a true fellowship of ministry. Or PASTOR/STAFF can mean a time of heartache, personal pain, intimidation, and a failing ministry.

Some of the most delightful spiritual experiences and times of fellowship have come to me through the leadership and friendship of former pastors. The team concept is still a goal of the church staff. It is a wonderful experience when the church staff are good friends as well as "religious leaders"!

Before we get too deep into church staff relations, let's talk about the call of God in the life of the music minister. When I was a high school youngster, with no background in music or spiritual things, God extended His call to me. It happened like this:

In the summer of 1954, I was at a Southern Baptist Convention Church Training Week in the mountains of Virginia. At the end of the final service, while sitting on the back row with some newfound friends, I heard the voice of God extend to this "rising senior" in high school an absolute and definite calling into the ministry of music as a vocation. I responded to that call, to the surprise of all my friends . . . and to my own surprise! I walked that aisle, took the preacher's hand, and told him that God had just called me into the ministry of music—full time!

Now there are some unusual things surrounding this calling:

- In 1954 the music ministry was a brand-new thing. There weren't but a precious handful of full-time music ministers all across our land! Why would the Father call a young man into a ministry that was so new that even the local church really did not understand what it was?
- I came from basically a nonchurch family background with a history of heavy alcoholism on both sides of my family tree; so why would the Lord call a young high school student with this background into a new ministry?
- I had no musical skills whatsoever. I could play no instrument. I did not have a pleasing solo voice. I never had any music lessons. Why would the Lord call a nontalented young man into His service in an area that required basic skills?

I don't know the answers to these questions. But I do remember vividly the call of God on my life on that hot summer evening in Virginia.

I did finish high school and graduated from Oklahoma Baptist University as a music major. Then I attended Southwestern Baptist Theological Seminary, Fort Worth, Texas, and graduated with a double major in theory and composition.

That gives you some idea of my background. Each of you could give your own testimony, sharing how God called you into His ministry. This is important—that you know your calling and translate that into the implementation of your ministry.

The PASTOR is really the CEO (Chief Executive Officer) of the church. Usually a church extends a call to the PASTOR to lead the church in spiritual matters and to oversee the church staff. In addition to his ministry in the pulpit, sermon preparation, visiting, and all the other things a PASTOR does, he is also responsible for leading the current staff and the lay leadership, who have also been called—to be members of that specific church and to have those specific responsibilities in the church program. The STAFF is responsible, ultimately, to the PASTOR.

And there is a most important area to consider at this time: Does the calling of the PASTOR and the calling of other STAFF members "mesh," fit, work, feel comfortable?

If God has called a person into the ministry, only God can call him out of the ministry. If God has led a person to move to a new church situation, and if the church has felt this call of God for the church and for the individual, only God will know when it is time for this person to move to a new field. God—and only God—has the right and privilege to move a staff member to a new situation. But part of the leadership of the Holy Spirit in the life of a STAFF member might be a dawning realization that their two styles of ministry do not go together . . . do not fit . . . do not work . . . and are poles apart in concept and implementation!

Suppose the music minister, for example, has been at the church for eight years and has a rather successful program, but not the kind of program the new PASTOR desires. This new PASTOR comes on the scene and should counsel and encourage this music minister to consider a different direction in his program. After a certain amount of time has passed, and after continuing conversations between PASTOR and music minister, if the concepts of worship, music, and ministry still are far apart, it behooves the minister of music to begin seeking the will of God in another church field. Remember: The church has called the PASTOR to be the CEO and to build the church through his own leadership and personality. If other STAFF cannot go along with the program, they should be looking to move.

This does not interrupt the call of God in their lives; it only challenges them to be open to the leadership of the Holy Spirit when personalities, philosophies, and concepts do not go together as smoothly as one might wish. Most staff ministers will be open to discussion with committees about their work, their responsibilities, and their futures. Most will take it under consideration to begin praying for the Lord to lead them to a new field that will complement their ministry. Most will appreciate the careful handling of a very delicate situation. Most will probably move to a new field of service soon, and with the blessing of the church family. How much sweeter the feelings when things are handled according to the Scriptures.

As the passage in 1 Corinthians 12:4-5 says, there are differences of administration, but the same Lord. STAFF members can and should work together in harmony for the same goal. Each may have a different way of doing a task, but the ultimate goal should be the same.

There are areas of ministry in which the STAFF can encourage and guide each other. For instance, it is interesting that the PASTOR, for the most part, does not take any classes in graduate-level seminary in the "art of worship." Other staff members are required to take "worship" as part of the degree program, but not the PASTOR. This is a tragedy! The PASTOR is the one whom the congregation looks to for leadership in worship—and yet he has had no background in the art of worship. What a great opportunity for the STAFF! Seminars, discussions, concepts, and encouragements can be offered to each other as the staff, in one accord, seek to learn about the concepts of worship and how to plan and implement the worship experience for their own congregation.

Most pastors will be open to learning with the staff that there is more to a worship experience than the sermon and the invitation. (More on WORSHIP in a later chapter.)

Certainly the PASTOR should be the leader, the person in charge of the STAFF, the person to whom the STAFF looks for leadership. The PASTOR can give away some of this responsibility to administrators and/or others in STAFF leadership positions, but the PASTOR who does not regularly come to STAFF meetings and have an active and vital part in the business of administering the program of the church and a part in the fellowship of the STAFF will lose sight of his STAFF and live in his own dream tower. The STAFF can help keep each other humble and real. The STAFF can offer input to each other's programs. The STAFF can minister to each other. Everyone needs someone—and this includes the PASTOR. Pastors need friends too—and STAFF members make good friends.

The church STAFF should be good friends with each other, if at all possible. These STAFF members should feel free to invite each other to dinner, for fellowship after church, for outings. The STAFF members should feel free to communicate and fellowship with the PASTOR and his family. The PASTOR should not be treated as a "sub-God" and never treated as a human being—for he is, first and foremost, a human being, with a built-in need for fellowship with humankind.

The STAFF should play together often . . . playing golf or racquetball or tennis . . . eating lunch together once in a while. This fellowship among STAFF will show up positively during Sunday services and other church activities. The STAFF that is really a team is a delight to experience—and it makes the church family feel comfortable, pleased, and secure.

STAFF retreats are a must, especially if the STAFF is a large one—more than three! These times of getting away from the phone, from the minor things of the day, to concentrate on praying together for the church, the calendar for the coming six months or year, details of each ministry, laughing and eating together—these times will pay great dividends in the total ministry of the church for the community.

STAFF members should not talk about each other to church members—except in the positive! Nothing negative should be communicated to church members. This is common courtesy to the STAFF member. If you have a problem with another STAFF member, take him on face to face and do not run a campaign behind his back. STAFF members should be frank and honest with each other—to the point and blunt at times. Be able to agree and disagree with each other without anger. Be able to take constructive criticism from your peers.

Here are ten ways to earn STAFF and self-respect—and maybe the confidence of a PASTOR.

1. *Respect yourself.* Know your strengths and weaknesses. Know who you are and what you are capable of doing. Do not be intimidated by other STAFF, church members, or peers. Be confident in your calling, your skills, and your position.

2. *Give credit where credit is due.* Be lavish in giving away applause. One of the great conductors of our time

is Robert Shaw, formerly the musical director/conductor of the Atlanta Symphony Orchestra. Shaw rarely accepts applause for himself. He is always having the soloists stand, the orchestra stand, the concertmaster stand, the choir stand, the soloists take a bow . . . but he only rarely will take a full bow for himself.

Tell the choir or congregation that your secretary did this report, and brag on how efficient it is. Tell the choir what a good job the officers are doing. Compliment your soloists often. Brag on your accompanists and instrumentalists. Tell the congregation how pleased you are with their response to the hymns and how well they are singing. Write "love notes" all the time to people.

3. *Don't become too familiar with your people.* This is very difficult for church STAFF people. All of us want to have friends and to be wanted, but some of us go too far and become too friendly and too familiar with church people. This will lead to a hard fall. Just be careful and space your friendships out so you don't require just one very close and personal friend to see you through the day.

4. *Criticize in private; commend in public.* We have discussed this earlier in this chapter. Do not allow your comments in public to be negative—only positive.

5. *Observe all the rules you expect everyone else to observe.* Just because you are STAFF, you cannot come and go as you please, with no clock or schedule. If other staff members pay for Wednesday dinners, you pay for Wednesday dinners. If they have fifteen-minute coffee breaks, you take fifteen-minute coffee breaks.

6. *Don't make threats or promises you can't fulfill.* You have to be very careful here to watch yourself in conversation. Do not promise the moon and deliver only a twinkle. If you promise a raise to someone and it

doesn't come through, you are left hanging with no excuses. If you say you'll resign unless the budget is pledged—watch out!

7. *Respect confidences.* This is so important with church members and with friends. People will trust you if they know you won't divulge their confidences. Keep their trust by not telling their story from the pulpit, minus their names!

8. *Be consistent.* Don't allow yourself to be one way today and another way tomorrow! Be consistent in the pulpit, in rehearsals, in staff meetings, in committee meetings. Watch being moody. Watch bringing your burdens in for everyone to share.

9. *Keep calm under trying circumstances.* There are times when you will want to run and hide—but you can't. There are times when you will desire to resign—but you can't. There are times when you will want to fire someone—but you can't. There are times when you will want to walk out of a committee meeting in protest—but you can't. There are times when you will want to scream—but you can't. You *can* keep cool, calm, collected, and exude confidence. And people around you will catch it.

10. *Show enthusiasm and pep for your job.* This is a must! You cannot expect your people to be enthusiastic if you are not enthusiastic. Be happy, bright, friendly, confident, secure; and these features will be catching. Do your job with great pleasure—even the dirty parts of it. As they say, "Someone has to do it!" And it has to be you, so enjoy it. Don't be afraid to accept a new job, a new assignment, a new responsibility. There is great adventure in doing something new and exciting.

A recent survey of ninety outstanding, "world-class" men and women, all making over $500,000.00 per year, found these people all had four things in common:

- Each had a vision; they were dreamers.

- Each communicated well with people.
- Each was persistent in achieving his dreams.
- Each had a healthy self-respect.

On the other hand, a survey of one hundred persons who were in mental institutions revealed three interesting things that were common to all:

- Each lived in the past . . . dealt only with the past.
- Each one did not laugh very much.
- Each felt he never did anything right.

In which of these two surveys do you fall? Do you have a vision? Do you live in the past? Is it time for a personal survey?

And finally, there are seven basic styles of leadership that can be applied to church STAFF members. This material comes from a paper prepared by Mark Short, Jr.

1. *Autocratic or Controlling Leadership*—being in full and complete control of everything . . . knowing when everything happens, why it happens, and to whom it happens. This is a heart-attack style of leadership. It will eventually kill you.

2. *Bureaucratic Leadership*—well-oiled and smooth leadership . . . everything in its place with no questions asked. "Everything is cool" leadership style.

3. *"Yes Sir!" Leadership*—always saying yes to everything and to everybody, offending no one and keeping everyone happy by telling one group one thing and another group something else . . . just to keep them happy.

4. *Gamesman Leadership*—the "white horse" STAFF member who rides in to "save the church" and begins big programs costing lots of money. When people begin to complain and fuss, he rides off into the sunset to begin his work anew with another church.

5. *Laissez-faire Leadership* (or "hands off because

this is not my area")—will not do anything that isn't in the job description.

6. *Company Man Leadership*—never misses a denominational meeting, even if his own church is dying. He keeps up the good front—everything is fine here, as the church slowly sinks in the sunrise.

7. *Participatory Leadership*—with love and care. He is able to get along with people and loves to be with them, sharing in their hurts and successes.

People do things for their reasons, not ours. We simply help them learn to motivate themselves. Programs that "fold" when a STAFF member has departed have been the wrong kind of programs. These are programs that are successful because of one person; and when that person is gone, no one is left to hold up the timbers! This is poor leadership and will fail miserably. A STAFF member should multiply himself so that when he does leave, a program can continue and be somewhat healthy till another STAFF member can pick up the slack.

There are differences of administration; but the same Lord is over all of us who serve on the church STAFF. No matter how large or how small the STAFF, a cooperative leadership style needs to prevail and a spirit of love and fellowship needs to permeate the staff. God bless the STAFF members of all local churches. The job is hard and the earthly rewards few, but the final reward is something else to behold! Praise God!

Q
Quality

". . . presenting your offering at the altar . . ." (Matt. 5:23).

QUALITY. The very word exudes the finest, the best, the choicest of the choice. From the very beginning of creation, God has required the firstborn, the firstfruits, the first and the best of the cattle, the "lamb without blemish." God requires nothing less from us today. He is still God, and we are still His people. He is still "I am that I am," and we are still His chosen ones. We are to bring to Him the best we can offer. This extends into our worship (which we will cover later) and into the music we offer to Him in forms of praise and thanksgiving.

QUALITY does not necessarily mean Bach, Brahms, Beethoven, Chopin, Handel, and the other great masters from another time. QUALITY does not necessarily mean Gaither, Smith, Tunney, and the other contemporary writers.

QUALITY does mean the absolute best we can prepare and offer to God in our worship service with the resources at our disposal as music ministers. Remember: The congregation is *not* the audience; God is the audience. Our gifts of music and celebration are for His ears. Our congregations are to be led to be the "performers" in the worship experience, with the staff acting as prompters, encouragers. It is God we are attempting to please with our gifts of music—not the congregation, the pastor, the music committee, or the choirs. No, it is God, and God alone.

The music minister must carefully balance his/her selections of music to balance the likes and dislikes of the congregation, and of course, the likes and dislikes of the pastor. It is no easy road!

As was said earlier, a program cannot exist on one kind of music. Too much Bach in a service and over a period of time is as wrong as giving too much of the contemporary writers. God did not intend for a church family to have to worship to one kind of music all the time! One cannot grow and stretch unless one tackles something that challenges the mind. The same thing applies to the Scriptures, doesn't it? It would be so nice and comfortable to just have John 3:16 or the Sermon on the Mount preached to us on a regular basis. We would bask in the love of God and never be challenged to be good stewards, to be good witnesses, to be good soldiers of the cross, to be lighthouses in our communities, to be salt in our communities. We would just learn about the love of God and that's all.

But as the Christian life has many avenues and many adventures to challenge the Christian, so music has many colors and sounds to challenge the musician and the congregations. Again, the music minister must be a "middle of the road" person, using the best of all the avenues available to him in music. In the process, he can minister to the vast majority of his people.

When the music minister is instructed that from now on, he/she will only prepare and sing one kind of music, this is wrong! This is not the Christian way! This is a demand that should be unacceptable. As music ministers, we have to be sensitive to the musical needs of our congregation, just as the pastor is sensitive to the spiritual needs of the congregation. Many times the two needs (spiritual/musical) combine to aid each other and to bring about renewal.

A choir should not be made to prepare only music that is fast and loud and consists of a text that would not challenge the congregation to do anything but pat the foot. A choir should not be made to prepare only music that is somber, over two hundred years old, and has a text that is lost in another era. A choir should be challenged by the music minister, through cooperation with the pastor, to prepare music that would be uplifting to the congregation, that would lift up the name of God, uphold Christ, and challenge Christians to live above themselves. Walk a wide stream of musical tastes for your congregation, with as much QUALITY as is available to the resources before your people. Anything less is a cheap offering to God, His church, and His people.

QUALITY is not an alternative. It is a command from the Lord Himself. We are bound by His Word to bring to Him the best of our abilities, our music, our education, our preaching, our own gifts. We should be able to prepare freely with the resources available to us the very best in gospel music, classical music, contemporary music, spirituals, folk music, and more! God is not through with music yet and won't be till Jesus comes again. And as ministers, we are bound to give back to the Father what He has given us to use as resources in our own churches.

Won't it be interesting to hear what the angel Gabriel will play on his trumpet when he summons God's people home? Wonder if it will be a chorale . . . a song with a contemporary feel . . . a spiritual . . . a gospel song? Who knows? No one knows; and until Jesus comes again, we need to be offering to God all the best that is within us and within our peoples—a wide diversity of gifts, of music, of instruments, of singing, of preaching, of giving, of education, of everything that is good.

QUALITY belongs to the Lord!

R
Rehearsals

". . . who will prepare your way . . ." (Matt. 11:10).

REHEARSAL . . . ideally, a meeting of musicians (and singers) for the purpose of becoming familiar with music. In fact, someone has said that REHEARSALS are a social occasion where little, if any, real musical work is done! REHEARSAL . . . most useful for the repetition of mistakes. More often than not, this is true.

REHEARSAL should be one of the highlights of the week for those who participate in the choir. REHEARSAL should be stimulating, exciting, innovative, and creative. The people who attend should go away feeling glad they came. REHEARSALS should be well planned. REHEARSALS should be interesting. REHEARSALS should be fast-paced. REHEARSALS should *not* be boring!

Psalm 150 tells us to use everything imaginable to praise the Lord; and if we don't do it, the rocks and the mountains will clap their hands together to praise Him. Those who have chosen choir as an avenue of service to the Father are praising Him through their music—and this includes REHEARSALS—which puts a great deal of pressure on the music minister to ensure that these REHEARSALS include all the things mentioned above.

Some of the responsibility of REHEARSAL rests with the choir members too! Here are four avenues of responsibility that the choir has to God, the Father.

1. *Faithfulness.* Blessed is the music minister who has a choir that comes to REHEARSALS week by week, regular as clockwork, save emergency or job/family requirement. They come whether it is hot or cold, rain or shine, ball game or no ball game, mad or happy, early or late . . . they come to choir.

How frustrating it is to have prepared and planned an exciting, innovative rehearsal, sent out cards, made calls and visits, placed balloons on the chairs and candy in the seats—and have twenty-four of forty-five show up! Ever been there? We all have been there, and every choir has attendance problems. And most of the excuses or reasons are valid.

It is very frustrating to the music minister to want to teach a new anthem or to begin on a new Christmas work and have a bit more than half the choir present—and he has to reteach the same music next week to another group of people!

Here are some suggestions for your consideration that may make REHEARSALS a bit more interesting and exciting for your choir:

- Have the proper music in the choir folder. Make sure everyone has his/her own copy of music!
- Have the choir room a comfortable temperature and see that the room is clean, the chairs are in place, and the evening's REHEARSAL agenda is on the board and in order.
- If you have a weekly choir paper, put it in the folder slot or on the chair. Don't make any announcements in the choir rehearsal; let the choir paper take care of that detail or have the choir president handle announcements at the end of rehearsal.
- If you have refreshments, see that everything is

ready at least half an hour before rehearsal is to begin. Most choirs have a large number of people who cannot make prayer meeting due to job or family, and they arrive in time to have a cup of coffee and some fellowship. Someone needs to be present to greet them, share with them, and have a cup of coffee with them prior to rehearsal. Some of the most effective ministry can be done during this time. Sometimes cakes, cookies, and cold drinks are available before rehearsal. There should not be a rehearsal break, so eating and drinking must be done before or after. This promotes good fellowship and times of ministry to each other.

- Begin on time—every time—and end on time—every time! It is not fair for the REHEARSAL to begin ten minutes late to wait on five or seven people, when there are choir members in the room ready to go to work! So go to work! Begin the rehearsal with something familiar, in a good register for the voices, so as to warm up gently. But begin on time!

- Work fast, work hard, and keep them busy at all times, not giving time for whispering, jokes, or prolonged conversation. Switch around the music—beginning on page 5, second score, third measure, and work that section a while. Then go on to something else. Keep them on their toes, never letting them guess where you will begin or what section you will work. Keep ahead of them.

- When finished with the REHEARSAL plan, even if it's not 9:00, *quit*! Turn the REHEARSAL over to the president, and go sit down and let him/her complete REHEARSAL with prayer requests, a devotional thought, any announcements, and a closing prayer.

REHEARSALS that are consistently stimulating, interesting, refreshing, innovative, challenging, exciting, humorous, spiritually beneficial, and not boring will entice the choir to come—on time as much as possible, and consistently, for fear that if they miss a rehearsal, they might miss something exciting.

People will come for a quality program. If what is being offered is first-rate, first-class, and top-of-the-line, people will want to be involved in it and be a vital part of it!

2. *Attitude.* The attitude of the choir about their church, the worship services, and REHEARSAL is extremely important. It determines how they will react to given situations. It will affect their actions in REHEARSAL. You can't always control their attitudes because a flat tire on the way to church . . . or a three-year-old son getting in the charcoal bag in his new white suit . . . or a skinned knee on the bike before walking out the door for REHEARSAL will certainly put a damper on a good spirit. Attitudes play an important part in a rehearsal. Why are some rehearsals "electric" in feeling and the amount of work done . . . and some rehearsals the "pits"? It depends on the weather, the long day at work or play, the children, the confrontation immediately prior to choir, and much more!

Our responsibility as music ministers is to make that REHEARSAL the most exciting event of their day. And so we should!

3. *Responsibility.* Responsibility goes with faithfulness, but one can be faithful and not responsible. Being responsible means carrying out the task you have chosen for yourself. All choirs have choir members who are faithful but who lack responsibility. This is the choir member who always cuts up in rehearsals, draws attention to himself, never listens to instructions, is always late and never early, never has the right music, is always asking, "What page?" and gets in line and discovers he has no hymnal, while trying to put on his

robe and walk and get a bulletin at the same time! He may be faithful, but not responsible.

Responsibility is an awesome word, especially when it carries a relationship to the Father. Here are some guidelines that might be of interest to you as you consider responsibility in the choir for your people. Ask them:

- to be faithful in attendance to REHEARSALS and performances as much as is within their power; to take REHEARSALS seriously.
- to be in their place and ready before beginning time of the rehearsal to have a little peace of mind.
- to have the right folder, with the right music, a pencil, and a smile on their face.
- to listen carefully and make the time worthwhile for them and those around them.
- to be supportive of the music minister, the accompanist, the music sung, and their part in the worship experience.
- to use the right to disagree with the music minister, but not in public, in a rehearsal. Do that privately.
- to be willing, time permitting, to serve on choir committees, to be an officer, committed to doing a good job and not to accept anything unless they can fulfill it to the best of their abilities.
- to realize that their service to the choir and this church is a commitment to God.

4. *Commitment.* A commitment is a bond between you and whomever you are committing to. You have a commitment to your mate. You have a commitment to your job. You have a commitment to your church and to your work. You have a commitment to the choir, if you have chosen to be a member of this group. Perhaps not enough is said to prospects and new members about what is expected of them in choir—or in church, for that matter! We are so anxious to get them in that we

forget to tell them about the responsibilities that go with this commitment! We sometimes get so caught up in evangelism—the winning of new people—that we neglect the teaching and training of those whom we have won. They may become spiritually weak from neglect and drop away. We are prone to "win 'em and leave 'em!" An up-front commitment should also have an up-front explanation of what is expected.

Give them an opportunity to "try it" for a few rehearsals before "signing on" and let them see if the schedule or the time is going to be a problem before signing the dotted line for membership in the choir.

A good rule of thumb is to encourage at least three visits in rehearsal before they sign up. This will let them confront good times and not-so-good times, meet different people in the choir, see how the choir family reacts to different situations, and have enough time to make up their minds. Then when they do commit, they will be good, faithful members.

Let them know that you understand that it is hard to leave that fireplace on a cold, rainy night, to leave the TV screen when your team is about to win, or to go out after a good, hot, enjoyable meal at home after a hard day's work! But at the same time, they made a commitment, and people are counting on them. They need the rehearsal to be prepared for the coming events, and they need to fill their seat and be found faithful. The embers of the fire are better later in the evening, anyway!

REHEARSALS should be musical, humorous, and spiritual. We have loads of music—up to ten anthems per REHEARSAL. We have lots of fun with each other. We love each other and we care for each other. And the spiritual side will be interpreted through the music, the texts, and the love that is shared in the rehearsal time.

Now to the more personal side of REHEARSAL. The music minister has the sole responsibility for a successful REHEARSAL. If it falls apart, if it is terrible, if it has no spark or drive, you have to accept full responsibility! Evaluation sometimes helps put the REHEARSAL in good perspective. Why was it a bad rehearsal? What factors contributed to the failure? Was it a total failure—or just where did it break down? Did you have full control of the rehearsal, or did you sense it being taken from you with the talking, the humor, the jokes, and the lack of concentration on the part of the choir members? What can you do to prevent this from happening again? How was the rehearsal paced? Was there too much new music . . . too much old music? Was one section the cause of the problem? Was one person the cause of the problem? Was time wasted?

The music minister should know his REHEARSAL plan inside and out . . . know exactly what he wishes to accomplish and set out to do just that, with nothing standing in the way.

Remember: People will come out for QUALITY. If your music ministry is a QUALITY program, and if you are doing your very best to praise the Father through music, to give a wide variety of literature, to ensure that your REHEARSALS are first-class, innovative, exciting, fast-paced—and if the choir members feel they accomplish something in the process—they will return over and over again! But the success or failure of the REHEARSAL rests solely and directly with the music minister.

One more time . . . from the beginning!

S

Sopranos

" . . . hosanna in the highest . . . " (Mark 11:10).

SOPRANO . . . the highest vocal line sung by women. SOPRANO . . . derived from the Latin word *superius*, which means "highest"—and as someone has said, this has given them a superiority complex, completely unfounded! SOPRANOS . . . have a tendency to sing sharp. SOPRANOS . . . faithful, quiet, and responsive. SOPRANOS . . . usually the largest section.

Every choir has an abundance of SOPRANOS, for if persons think they can't read music, they automatically sing SOPRANO. This also makes the SOPRANOS the poorest sight-reading section in a choir because in most music SOPRANOS sing melody.

SOPRANOS love to hit those high notes—the higher, the better. Most of them are hit rather well!

Unusual things are found in the choir folders of SOPRANOS: hat pins (they still make those?), bobby pins, hankies, breath mints (now we know!), melted chocolate bars, bulletins from the last three years, every note they have ever gotten in choir, two or more red pencils, all without points . . . and the music. Their choir music is well marked, in response to their director's instructions, but some of them can't spell! Recently a director was telling the SOPRANOS to crescendo and to write it in their music. One SOPRANO wrote it in the right place but spelled it "Kirsendough"!

SOPRANOS are the mainstay and foundation of every choir. They are the first in their seats . . . the first with their music open . . . the first section ready to sing . . . and the first section to volunteer for anything. Directors count on SOPRANOS. A choir with a good SOPRANO section is a choir with depth and security. An insecure SOPRANO is like a deflating balloon. There is something missing—breath support and air!

Most SOPRANOS have had music lessons, and many have had voice lessons. Good SOPRANOS bring a certain musicianship to the choir family, an air of security and purpose. They are hard workers, anxious to get the notes correct and angry at themselves and at the music minister if they do not succeed. SOPRANOS are quick to call attention to a mistake by the director—any mistake!

In a recent conference the lecturer said that SOPRANOS blend as a section only when required to do so. They have the capabilities to blend, but do not work at it very hard unless reminded and pushed to listen to the other SOPRANOS.

SOPRANOS are hard workers. Like the ALTOS, they volunteer to do things and usually do them very well. Some of the best choir presidents are SOPRANOS. They have a knack for detail and organization (except in their choir folders) and enjoy a leadership position in the choir family.

SOPRANOS are usually firm supporters of the music minister. They defend him/her strongly in public, even though they may disagree with him/her privately. This is commendable and is appreciated.

SOPRANOS usually tend to remain in choir as long

as possible, till they are up in years! This is a good testimony of their dedication and love for the choir and this avenue of service to God through music.

SOPRANOS—one of four sections—but a section with strength, maturity, musicianship, good attitudes, and a choir folder full of junk! Every choir needs a good dose of SOPRANOS!

T
Tenors

"Glory to God in the highest . . . " (Luke 2:14).

Someone said that TENORS come in two categories. The first is just "plain TENORS," a high-pitched adult male voice, who much prefers singing in the middle register and gently soaring to the upper extremes, sometimes rather loudly, when everyone else is singing softly. "Plain TENORS" are not found in great numbers in any choir; so many times, frustrated baritones are asked to sing the TENOR line. Then we have baritones, who can't reach the high notes, and the TENORS, who don't like to sing the lower notes, giving the director an indication that perhaps accounting would have been a better vocation.

COUNTERTENORS is the other category of TENOR. One person said that COUNTERTENOR is the highest adult male voice currently available through legal or moral means. He also said the COUNTERTENOR sings roughly in the range of the contralto, although he can sing lower if pressed . . . and higher, if pinched. COUNTERTENORS have a tendency to sing on pitch, but out of control. Must be the altitude up there!

TENORS are generally harassed by the BASS section of the choir. "Real men can't be TENORS!" they say! Well, it takes a real man to sing TENOR—especially with some of the high TENOR parts that some composers/arrangers write these days!

TENORS tend to be on time for rehearsals, hang their robes up neatly, and leave their coffee cups under the choir chair.

TENORS are willing to volunteer for duty when needed and generally follow through. TENORS like to take charge of rehearsal with cute remarks and verbal slaps at the BASSES and to make sure the music minister doesn't slip by with a mistake.

TENORS prefer to date ALTOS . . . but marry SOPRANOS. Because the TENOR section is usually the smallest section in a choir, TENORS have a tight fellowship and do not take to new members in their sections with quick acceptance. But once a new TENOR is accepted and proves his worth, he is a friend forever.

TENORS keep strange things in their choir folders. McDonald's Gift Certificates, love notes, birthday cards, a year's supply of Sunday bulletins, music from as far back as 1967, breath mints, breath spray, gum, and chocolate. When confronted by all this mess, TENORS will blame the BASSES for putting this stuff in their folders.

TENORS tend to doze in the worship service each Sunday about 11:46 a.m. TENORS will drop a hymnal in the service and look to the SOPRANO section, as if they did it!

TENORS are hard workers. They make good choir officers. They sing very loud but can be controlled if the director is a disciplinarian, works on "blend" with the choir on a regular basis, and carries a can of "TENOR mace" when they get out of hand or out of line.

TENORS are the butt of many jokes, such as this one:

A Texan died and went to heaven. Peter asked him what he would like to do first since he had made it to heaven. The Texan said he'd like to form a choir. Peter said that would be fine; they needed one more choir. The Texan asked for one thousand SOPRANOS, eight hundred ALTOS, and six hundred BASSES. "What about TENORS?" asked Peter. "Don't need any!" said the Texan. "I'll sing TENOR."

U
Unknown

" . . . as unknown yet well-known . . . " (2 Cor. 6:9).

There are many, many UNKNOWN factors involved in the music ministry and in every walk of life. Many people fear the UNKNOWN. Others enjoy being able to explore the UNKNOWN. Every minute of every day is UNKNOWN, so we live with the unknown daily.

Part of the UNKNOWN is your own personal acceptance in the world of music. Having taught freshman music theory at Samford University, Birmingham, Alabama, for nine years, I had exposure to many college freshmen each year who were majoring or minoring in music and seeking a direction in their lives. Many came to major in music who were not really qualified to do so. After some personal counseling, these students would confide in me that they were the number one musician in their little church back home and that everyone had said to them for years that they should be a music minister, for God had given them such a good voice or piano ability. But when they arrived on campus, they were in a pool of 150 music majors/minors who were every bit as good as or better than they were. The competition was beginning to show them that perhaps another vocation would be acceptable.

Many of them told me they had to major in music

because Mom and/or Dad expected this and they were paying the bills. "But what if this is not what *you* want to do with your life?" I would ask. "I don't have the guts to tell them I am not happy being a music major or music minor," they would tell me.

They feared the UNKNOWN . . . the getting out into the real world! They feared the UNKNOWN of telling their parents that maybe God had not called them into the music ministry. They feared the UNKNOWN of telling their little home church that perhaps God had other opportunities for them out there besides music.

Being accepted in the world of music is a difficult task, even if you are very good and very talented and very secure. But if you have your own personal doubts about your calling, then it is doubly difficult to achieve this acceptance with peers. Musicians and people related to the fine arts tend to give the impression of being snobby, and sometimes this is true. Other times, it is being caught up in their own little private world, living in their own white tower, being oblivious to anything and anyone around them.

And yet even people dealing in the world of fine arts are fearful of the UNKNOWN . . . the UNKNOWN of knowing if your piece will be accepted for publication—your play produced, accepted, reviewed, closed—your painting banned—your sculpture accepted—and so on.

The UNKNOWN plays a big part in deciding which graduate school to attend . . . which professors to take . . . which courses to take. The UNKNOWN finds its way into your decision as to a life's vocation, especially in church work. Which church is right for me? Which church will challenge me to stretch and grow as I challenge them to stretch and grow? Will the pastor and I be good friends, or will there be struggles over styles and philosophies of music from day one? Will I like the choir and will the choir like me? All of this is UNKNOWN.

It spills over into every part of our lives, this UNKNOWN! It makes all of us uncomfortable. It makes all of us wary. It challenges the best of us to walk new ground, in spite of shaking knees.

Jesus promised that He would be with us, walk with us, guide us, direct us, nudge us along in His will . . . if we would be faithful to Him and to His cause. "I will never leave you, nor forsake you," He told us. We have to claim that promise, even in the midst of the UNKNOWNS of our lives. We have to keep our eyes fixed on Jesus and not fear the UNKNOWN, but walk boldly day after day, trusting in Him to give us guidance.

The UNKNOWN . . . an opportunity waiting!

V
Visitation

". . . and you visited me . . ." (Matt. 25:36).

VISITATION can either be an enjoyable adventure or a complete disaster. VISITATION can be part of your job description, or it can be something you do because you are a member of the church. VISITATION can be a vital part of your personal ministry, or you can be made to do it because it is in your job description.

I was a part-time minister of music/youth in a small church in Texas during Southwestern Seminary days. Traveling back and forth to seminary twice a week, keeping a semi-full program going at the church, planning the worship services, keeping up with correspondence, promotion, and other church-related activities, caring for a young bride, and doing three choir rehearsals was about all I could do and remain sane! This was, of course, in addition to graduate-level studies in the Master of Church Music degree!

I thought I had, in a part-time student position, no room for any other responsibilities. My pastor, however, thought I should also visit. We discussed it often, but I ended up visiting anyway! I was assigned one morning to visit a family of the church who were "fringe" members, whose mother, who lived with them, had just died. I was to make the "death call." I arrived at the same time the ambulance did. Here was this little seminary student, still wet behind the ears and having no idea what to say to strangers who did not know me or why I was there. I walked up and began talking to the bereaved. I was totally ignored. They wanted to speak with the pastor, not one of the other ministers—especially a part-time student minister of music.

I learned a valuable lesson from that traumatic experience and wish to share it with you. You will recognize that I have strong feelings in this area, and I do not expect all readers to agree with me. Nevertheless, I want to share my concerns with you. Obviously, what I recommend will have to be adapted to the size of church you serve.

It is the place and responsibility of the pastor to minister to the entire church family, with help and assistance from other ministerial staff and dedicated, godly laypeople.

It is the place of the other ministerial staff to minister to persons involved in their areas of responsibility—persons whom they know and who know them.

The other ministers should visit newcomers who can fit into their particular ministries. For instance, the music minister should visit any newcomers who have interests in the arts, who have children of any age, and who have the skills to be involved in the music ministry. The same thing goes for the youth minister; he visits those newcomers who have children/youth and who have the skills to fit into the youth program.

I have visited young couples who had no interest whatsoever in music and wondered why the church sent the music minister to visit them instead of the children's minister. They worked with children in their previous church. So I gave their name to the children's minister. A second visit was made, and two valuable hours were spent visiting the same couple when one visit would have been sufficient—by the right staff member.

I have visited older people who have no interest whatsoever in music, who don't even like to sing and have never sung in a choir before. Why didn't the church send the director of the senior adult group to their home? That's what they are interested in!

Many times the pastors require all staff to spend one afternoon or one day in personal visitation, regardless. It is part of the job description and must be carried out.

If you are in this situation, there should be room for flexibility between ministers. For example, the music minister could spend his time ministering to his "choir flock." They get sick too. They have babies too. They need comfort and counsel too.

We ministers tend to ignore visiting those who participate with some degree of regularity. Sometime ask some of your people to honestly answer this question: "In the past year, has any member of the staff visited you, dropped you a note, or called you?" You will find that most of the time their answer will be no.

I feel that a valuable support ministry to the pastor's care of the total flock of the church can be gained by the various ministers keeping up with people in their particular ministries. Phoning, writing personal notes of thanks, appreciation, condolences, or dropping by to visit will free the pastor from having to do this and allow him to concentrate on those members of the flock who need pastoral care, those who are lost and need the Lord in the lives, and for personal visitation when an area of interest cannot be assigned to other ministers.

A music minister is usually much more comfortable ministering to his own sub-flock of people with whom he is familiar than visiting new people, who might be more appreciative of a personal visit from the pastor. More good can be accomplished by allowing the other ministers to visit people involved in their programs and relating needs to the pastor than merely passing out visitor's cards in weekly staff meeting and expecting a full report and "shoe size" by next week.

Every staff member has more to do than he can possibly do (or at least, he should!). Every staff member should use time in ways most effective for the church. I think VISITATION could be discussed at a staff retreat and some conclusions drawn that would make everyone feel at ease, useful, and comfortable. There is a better way to accomplish more in less time by all the staff ministers in VISITATION if the situations are discussed in dialogue with other staff and if the pastor is flexible enough to allow the staff team to have some say in the VISITATION policy.

There are ministerial staff who have the gift for visiting newcomers, who do like to grab a card and go! This is fine and there is absolutely no problem . . . if this staff member is also visiting and ministering to people within his realm of ministry.

These are tough words and sometimes tough words offend. That is not my intention here, but the intention is to make a strong point: VISITATION is like making a good pound cake. It takes lots of good ingredients to make it turn out right. The same is true with VISITATION. It takes all the ministerial staff working together, figuring out the best way to make the VISITATION process in the church the most effective . . . the best way to involve the minister of music in VISITATION that will be the most beneficial to him and to his program. The same is true of all the other ministers.

Then . . . you funnel back to the pastor those needs that require further pastoral care. It seems so easy.

W
Worship

". . . we . . . have come to worship Him . . ." (Matt. 2:2).

WORSHIP is the most important event that happens weekly in the local church. WORSHIP should be the event that binds together the church family. WORSHIP is the event that needs the concentrated prayer efforts of staff, deacons, and laypeople. WORSHIP is the one time per week when the great majority of laypeople are present for fellowship, Bible study, the giving of tithes and offerings, challenge, and commitment. WORSHIP is the time when everything should be at the best, the peak. WORSHIP occurs when challenge is given and hearts are made new.

WORSHIP is the event where some churches do not list hymns, special music, or sermon subjects. WORSHIP is the time that creeps up on staff and congregation alike and both find that time has run out for preparation; the event is upon us. WORSHIP is the time to pull out an old "sugar stick" anthem or a "warmed-over sermon" and give it to the people, for we didn't have time to prepare something fresh. WORSHIP is a time to be careful not to offend any of the brothers or sisters in the congregation. WORSHIP is the one time of the week to nap or doze because the music/sermon is boring . . . boring . . . boring.

Both of these paragraphs are true. WORSHIP can be both sublime and boring. How can we ensure that the WORSHIP experience will be one of discipline, care, beauty, and meaningfulness? It is very difficult, but it can be done. Here are some vital suggestions, not listed in any particular order of importance.

1. *WORSHIP requires discipline.* The discipline of WORSHIP requires that the staff lead the people to understand that WORSHIP is important, is to be taken seriously, and is not an easy responsibility. WORSHIP requires personal discipline on the part of every person in the service, including every staff member and all those who have an active part in the service. Persons who participate in a WORSHIP service should never do so lightly. They should be aware that their responsibility in this service, the high point of the week, is high and holy. WORSHIP requires a holy discipline and a concern that the WORSHIP experience be one that draws people to the Father and gives them a personal encounter with the Creator.

2. *WORSHIP requires preparation.* Preparation for WORSHIP is an absolute necessity. Without preparation, WORSHIP is an event of lesser proportions ... an ego trip for the minister/staff ... something for the congregation to discuss in negative terms over Sunday lunch. The staff who does not prepare carefully and specifically for the WORSHIP experience is not vitally concerned with their flock. To expect a congregation to enter the sanctuary and automatically be ready for WORSHIP is as sound an idea as passing Hebrew on the seminary level without studying. Here are people from all economic levels, with and without children, various levels of education, backgrounds, skills ... and these people are coming into the sanctuary to WORSHIP the true and living God. Do we expect them to do this with just an order of service in their hands? The

fact that we have prepared an order of service does not mean we have prepared a service of WORSHIP! Nothing happens without previous preparation. The Spirit of God will probably not move on a congregation that is simply going through the motions of WORSHIP or playing the game of spending an hour with God. A congregation deserves the best preparation for the WORSHIP experience, and nothing less than our best preparation will do.

I was in a worship service recently with a room full of contemporary Christian musicians, all godly men and women who love the Lord and who are called into His service. The WORSHIP leader told us at the beginning that he was going to allow the Holy Spirit to take the service and do with it what He wished; we were just to move with the flow of the service.

Little actual preparation had been made. A gentleman led us in a half-hour of choruses that he had written, none of which the majority of the people present knew! Then a prayer time was called for. We had so many specific requests for individual prayer needs that they boggled the mind. How could we remember all those specific prayer requests? This took another twenty minutes. A couple of soloists were next, then a harpist. Personal testimonies were called for next. At 10:45 p.m. (this service began at 7:00 p.m.) I left, very discouraged at having worshiped very little. That service, I'm told, was over at 11:30 p.m.

Now four and one-half hours for a WORSHIP service—with no breaks—is too long. This service was not well planned. No one was in charge, carrying the authority to prepare carefully a service that could have been absolutely electric. Some of the very best Christian artists in the United States were present in that service, but were not included as WORSHIP leaders.

My heart was heavy because of the missed opportunity of exciting and stimulating WORSHIP.

The staff of the local church—in particular, the pastor and the music minister—must sit down weekly or monthly and discuss the WORSHIP service. Are there to be any additions? Who is to participate? Should the order of WORSHIP be changed in format? What will be the theme of these coming services? Who will write the responsive reading, if one is to be written? If not, from what source will the responsive reading be taken?

Some congregations do not have to worry about an order of WORSHIP because it is always the same order of WORSHIP. But many congregations do have the freedom to change and alter their services as frequently as they wish. This makes their services fresh and appealing. A WORSHIP service should be changed at least once a month to add freshness and vitality to the service. These do not have to be major changes, but something new needs to be present.

Orders of WORSHIP are good . . . and they are bad! They are good because they allow the people to see what is going to happen in the WORSHIP service (at least, those who do read it will see it!). They are good because having them makes the staff prepare the service carefully. They are bad because many churches will not depart from this printed service, no matter what. An order of WORSHIP is simply a guideline to what is to take place in the experience—nothing more, nothing less. Careful preparation will ensure a WORSHIP experience that will be meaningful to your people.

3. *WORSHIP requires participation.* I have in my files an order of worship for a morning service where the pastor's name appears fifteen times! It becomes humorous to read it. Every event of the service has the pastor's name on it! "Morning Prayer . . . Pastor" . . .

"Responsive Reading . . . Pastor," etc., etc. No one person should do everything in the WORSHIP service. The pastor, the staff, and the laypeople should all have active contributions to make.

The more participation you can have from the laypeople in your congregation, the more exciting and meaningful your service will be. But some pastors think they must make the announcements because the people will respond better if the pastor challenges them to do things. Some pastors lead in the responsive readings because they think the people will respond better if the pastor is the leader. Some pastors announce the hymns in the service because they feel the people will sing better if the pastor announces the hymns and encourages them to sing. This type of pastor does not have enough confidence in his staff or his people to allow them leadership opportunities.

The more lay leadership you can enlist to be a part of the WORSHIP service, the more personal the service will be for the congregation. Every ministerial staff member should have a part in the WORSHIP service. The people need to see their staff in WORSHIP leadership.

Spontaneity is a vital part of any WORSHIP experience. There should be times when things happen in the service that are not expected. Or even if these things are listed in the order of service, it does not tell them where or how they will take place. This is called "planned spontaneity." It is "spontaneity with rehearsal." It is "spontaneity with preparation."

Suppose a soloist is listed in the bulletin. Why does the soloist have to sing from the pulpit? Have the soloist sing from the fifth row, center section, turning toward the congregation as he/she sings. This soloist is part of the congregation and identifies with them as the song is presented.

Responsive readings . . . why always minister-congregation or minister-choir? Why not have individuals from the congregation reading back and forth with each other? This will add new meaning to this important feature of the service. If the handbells are to play for this service, let them play from the back of the auditorium, from the side, or from the balcony (assuming, of course, that your church has a balcony!). If there is to be a brass quartet that morning for the anthem, allow them to play on one of the hymns. Have each part standing in a different part of the sanctuary. This "planning" takes place prior to the service; but to the congregation, it looks like a spontaneous feature and will likely be well received. Always rehearse these added features of the WORSHIP experience.

4. *WORSHIP requires patience.* Patience is the crown of kings, and you need patience when you plan a WORSHIP experience. Your congregational participants may cancel on you at the last minute. They may show up late for the rehearsal. You may have to spend valuable time searching for the right person to fill a specific spot. You will need to require your organist/pianist and the brass players to come early and rehearse the hymn. You will need to make sure the bell tables are in place and out of the traffic pattern of your sanctuary. You will need to write letters explaining what you wish them to do, when, where, and why. And afterward you will want to write letters of appreciation, thanking them for their participation.

All of this takes patience and precious time. But someone has to do it. And to the one who does it, keeps his ego under control, and has no problem with other people having the spotlight, the reward will be a great feeling of personal satisfaction in knowing the WORSHIP experience went off smoothly, as planned and rehearsed.

Everyone has their own personal horror stories of WORSHIP experiences that have gone wrong for some reason or another. We've all had choirs march in at the wrong time or into the wrong place. One friend of mine tells the story of a children's choir that marched into the basement of the church, out the rear door, around the side of the church, and into the sanctuary—all by mistake—when they were simply to come in the side door! Someone new was leading and didn't know where to go, and no one was prepared to escort them to the right place!

Someone else tells the story of their adult choir marching through the baptistry (it was empty at the time) because a new TENOR, leading the choir into the loft, entered the wrong door; and everyone followed! Yet another person tells the horror story of a Christmas pageant done with professional lights, professional sound, and costumes. When the children were on the risers, the light bar started down ever so slowly. By the time the children finished singing, the light bar was almost touching the tops of their heads—obviously a mistake, but nothing could be done about it at the time! Someone goofed the cue and went too far.

The standard story comes to mind of the organist who gave the hymn introduction in four sharps, and the pianist, who always transposed everything to flats, came in on the first stanza in three flats! Preparation and patience were certainly needed for that situation!

We must remember that our church members are laypeople, not full-time staff members. They assist us because they desire to be a part of the WORSHIP service, not because they have to do it. And there is a certain freshness about people who do things because they *want* to be of service!

5. *WORSHIP requires creativity.* If your WORSHIP

services are boring and dull, then *you* and/or your pastor are responsible! The people will participate in the kind of service we prepare for them with the leadership of the Holy Spirit . . . and the Holy Spirit does not design boring WORSHIP services. In fact, in spite of our meager attempts to create exciting WORSHIP, the Holy Spirit does pretty well solo!

A WORSHIP service must have creativity attached to it. We live in the last of the twentieth century, almost into the twenty-first century; and many of our attempts to provide WORSHIP experiences for our people come from other centuries! We live in the age when almost everyone alive today has had television exposure since an early age. We have seen professionally produced programs of every kind since the cradle. We have been exposed to Broadway shows on tour in our cities. We have experienced community productions, symphony orchestras, great conductors, great singers. We have watched the best available. And if we didn't like it, we could "change the channel"!

Well, brothers and sisters, we can't change the channel in church—not physically. But our people change the channels on us mentally! If our services are not inspiring, creative, innovative, and up to date, they turn us off in their minds and begin counting the windowpanes, the pews, those on the right side, and the light bulbs that are out in the light fixtures!

We continue to do the same order of service that we did ten, fifteen, twenty years ago, and we wonder why our people don't participate. We sing the same old hymns, written for another generation, and we wonder why our people don't sing the hymns on Sunday. We sing the same anthems year after year and wonder why our choir isn't growing. We are afraid to change the sanctuary to get more seating for the growing choir.

And we wonder why things aren't happening in the kingdom of God?

WORSHIP demands the absolute best . . . the most creative services we can give our people. We must strive to bring our orders of WORSHIP into the twenty-first century or pay the consequences for lack of preparation and ingenuity.

6. *WORSHIP requires a commitment to the future.* I tour every summer with a group of high school and college young people called The Baptist Festival Singers. We tour in Germany, Austria, Switzerland, France, and England. One of the highlights of every tour is the visits to the wonderful cathedrals in each of these countries. They are beautiful. They are worshipful. They were built in other centuries, but are still inspiring.

But the most interesting fact is that they are basically empty! Only the very old and the very young go to church in Europe. These cathedrals were full to overflowing at one time, but they are now devoid of people. I imagine that WORSHIP was not the primary objective in another time; perhaps ritual was.

Look around us, dear ones! Look at the wonderful, huge, and beautiful worship centers we are building across the United States. Look at churches moving out of the downtown areas to get to the suburbs where the affluent people live. Look at the buildings that are being built, based on the personality of a pastor. Look at the "fortress church," providing the congregation's every need, without their having to go out of the fortress and deal with the real world.

Look at our congregations. Are they mostly middle-aged and senior adult people? Where are the vast numbers of teenagers, college students, young adults, young marrieds? What are they doing on Sunday mornings instead of being in a local church? But more importantly—*why* are they not in a local church on Sunday morning?

Survey your community and you will find young people and young married couples who do not like to go to church because, they say, it is boring. *Boring!* Does that surprise you? WORSHIP of the true and living God, the Creator of the universe, the Lord and Savior of mankind, the God who made our intricate bodies and gave us brains and the freedom to make our own decisions—this same God is ignored weekly by millions of people because our WORSHIP services are *boring!*

This needs to strike a chord somewhere in our inner minds and remind us that unless we get down from our spiritual hobbyhorses and meet the demands of the community in which we live, then our churches, too, will very soon be empty except for the very old and the very young.

"But my church is not like this in any way!" you say. Wonderful! There are some churches who are reaching out beyond themselves and the "church fortress" into the world and making a difference. But there are some churches who are led to commit themselves to huge building programs with huge debts, strapping themselves financially. As a result, they cut back on local and world missions, the feeding/housing of the hungry and homeless, and the cooperative efforts of their denominations. The money they give is earmarked to complete the building, while other church ministries become strapped for finances to run their programs for years to come.

You can't run attractive programs without financial assistance. The program that is not spending a little money is in neutral! The program that comes in month after month to church conference and brags that they did not spend any money this past month is a program that is losing ground and people! When churches cut back financially on other programs to concentrate great amounts of money into building buildings, saving money, paying off debts, and so forth, the educational programs will eventually suffer because of the pressure not to spend the monies necessary to keep an attractive program in high gear.

The church must have a commitment to the future. We cannot forever live in the past. More people are staying away from the church than are being attracted to the church—and this should speak loud and clear to us. But it doesn't! We aren't listening. We are too busy running our own little kingdom, building our special building, writing our books, working day and night, to see that we are in a fistfight with Satan and he is winning! He is attracting our young people. He is offering them a false salvation in exchange for their souls. We sing the old hymns and read ancient prayers. And we wonder why the church of Jesus Christ is not on the cutting edge of life! It should be obvious to us, but Jesus told us that we had "eyes but could not see and ears but could not hear." In a recent survey of a large number of churches, it was discovered that 95 percent of the things we are presently doing to reach people and bring them into our churches are *not* working!

If what is happening is not obvious to our pastors and church staff leadership, it certainly should be obvious to our church congregations and her leadership! But it is not. They blindly follow wherever they are led, with little or no argument.

If we are going to cause a turnaround in the spiritual life of the United States, in all denominations, in all cultures, and minister to the lives of people in our communities as well as our churches, we are going to have to make some absolute changes in the way we have church and the way we view WORSHIP. Without these changes, we are doomed to end up like the beautiful, empty cathedrals of Europe, ministering to tour groups from abroad who visit the sanctuaries!

When will this change, this creative turnaround, come to pass? When the lay leadership of our local church say "enough is enough" and begin putting pressure on pastors and other ministerial staff to look to the future and not dwell in the past? Laypeople will be the answer to this dilemma, as they have been the answer to other spiritual dilemmas in religious history. Laypeople must understand that in order to bring people into our sanctuaries for WORSHIP, and in order to witness to them and share the good news of the gospel with them, we must update and remodel our attitudes toward WORSHIP. We must consider the following things:

- singing hymns that speak to contemporary issues;
- providing music that speaks to today's musical tastes, as well as to the past—using a wide variety of musical styles to appeal to the broader sector of the congregation;
- writing responsive readings and prayers that speak the language of the people;
- rethinking the concept of WORSHIP and its effect on the lives of those who come week after week . . . and those who seldom come at all;
- using more laypeople in the WORSHIP celebrations;
- beginning to be creative in the WORSHIP celebrations;
- changing the order of WORSHIP often to appeal to various age groups;
- having lots of congregational involvement in the service, so they will have a more active part as a congregation—instead of being "prayed for . . . sung to . . . and preached at";

- planning to "theme" the services and build everything around that theme;
- being bold to rethink the pulpit area/choir loft and other sanctuary areas that are dated, too small for a growing program; and be bold to change these for the betterment of the program;
- electing mature young people to places of church leadership and let them grow in the wisdom of the more mature leaders of the church;
- presenting WORSHIP—creative, stimulating, and bold—as the watchword of the church.

"And we have come to WORSHIP Him." That is the goal—to present the gospel of the Lord so that people can echo the words of the Wise Men.

Listen to the words concerning WORSHIP from God's Word:
- "WORSHIP the Lord with reverence" (Ps. 2:11).
- "WORSHIP the Lord in holy array" (Ps. 29:2).
- ". . . come and WORSHIP Him" (Matt. 2:8).
- ". . . fell down and worshiped Him" (Matt. 2:11).
- "WORSHIP in the Spirit of God" (Phil. 3:3).
- ". . . performing the divine WORSHIP" (Heb. 9:6).
- "WORSHIP Him who lives forever" (Rev. 4:10).

X
X-tra Special

". . . for a child will be born to us . . ." (Isa. 9:6).

The sounds, smells, and emotions of an X-TRA SPECIAL season give us the happiest, most joyous celebration of all—the birth of Christ, our Lord, in a stable, born to a virgin named Mary, and celebrated by Wise Men from the East and lowly shepherds from the hillside.

The X-TRA SPECIAL time of Christmas brings visions of sugarplums . . . brightly colored packages with bright bows . . . wonderful smells coming from the kitchen . . . visits with family, friends, children . . . the smell of fresh pine boughs . . . decorations . . . and best of all, the music of the season!

And this X-TRA SPECIAL season also brings to mind visions of missed entrances, children's choirs walking to the wrong place, dropped handbells, the clash of the cymbal in the wrong place, the fog machine not turning off and the whole stage being engulfed in fog so no one can see the director or the audience, bathrobed Wise Men, Mary with a baby doll to represent Jesus, and donkeys in the outdoor scene who wander off and make their presence known elsewhere!

Christmas is the season of seasons, especially for

Christian musicians! For we get to "live with" the music of the season for several months and completely absorb it, revel in it, and get from it every bit of pleasure possible—while our congregations only hear it once and may get only the barest amount of pleasure from the experience.

Christmas should be the most creative, celebrative, X-TRA SPECIAL event in our worship services during those holy days. Much time, thought, prayer, preparation, consideration, participation, and rehearsal should go into those services to make them the best we have to offer to the Christ child.

We should lead our people to high and holy hours in morning and evening worship. Beginning with the first Sunday of Advent, we should be celebrating, singing, reading, praying, processing, decorating, and more. We should be totally involved in the experience—not just the staff, the choirs, and the musicians, but the all of the congregation, young and old alike.

This X-TRA SPECIAL season gives the musicians more opportunity than any other season of the year to explore the rich possibilities of music in the services—all kinds of music, to suit and entice every taste.

We should sing the old carols, the ones that warm the inner beings of the soul. We should learn to sing new carols that speak of the birth celebration in contemporary language.

We should listen to instruments praise the Father with their tones. We should celebrate in our keyboard INSTRUMENTALISTS and their skilled fingers hard at work, playing rich and beautiful Christmas pieces. We should celebrate in the handbells and their ringing in the season of all seasons. We should thrill to the singing of the children—for this is a celebration that they can understand. They do not fully understand some other religious observances, but they do understand birth, in their own way. They understand tenderness from their parents, sharing from their family and friends, giving, and receiving.

Here are some suggestions as to what can be offered during this X-TRA SPECIAL season by the music ministry, in cooperation with others, and with the music ministry involved with the church family. Many of these you may have already tried, but you may also find a new idea here! Great!

- Every church can celebrate the season of Advent, beginning with Sunday I of Advent, and going through Sunday IV, which is the Sunday before Christmas. Many books give creative and innovative ideas for consideration about Advent, the lighting of the candles, the procession of the Advent participants, and much more. You can make this celebration as simple or as elaborate as you wish. It will take careful thought as to how to fit it into your order of worship, and it will take rehearsal! Never expect to do *anything* without rehearsal!

- Banners can be made depicting the season of Advent, and these can be brought down front in the worship service as part of the opening hymn, in a procession. Many books offer suggestions about how to make Advent banners. Any denominational book store will have an ample supply of such books.

- Congregational singing can be enhanced during this X-TRA SPECIAL season by the use of handbells, instruments, children, free accompaniments to Christmas hymns and variety in the singing, using choir-congregation, children-congregation, and any other combination that is comfortable in your church. Handbells, instruments, and/or children can be placed in the balcony, along the sides of the building, in the aisles, in the pews—anywhere that will add a change to

the service, excitement to the singing, and joy in the celebration.
- Choir specials during this X-TRA SPECIAL season can be chosen from an upcoming Christmas special production—selecting pieces from the musical, cantata, or special program, and singing all or portions of selected pieces—which will, of course, familiarize the congregation with the music. They will recognize it later on.
- The service choir for any given Sunday can be prepared to sing descants with the hymns. They can be prepared to sing creative endings to the hymns. They can be prepared to hold the endings longer than the congregation and instruments and have a separate cutoff (this is very exciting!). The service choir—or another choir—can be stationed in the narthex of the church and be singing as the people depart the sanctuary. This can all be worked out carefully in rehearsal.
- The X-TRA SPECIAL Christmas worship services can be full of very joyful music, using a variety of choirs, bells, and instruments as specials.
- The church choir or another service choir can be stationed in the narthex or another entrance to the sanctuary and be singing as the people enter for worship.
- A "Hanging of the Green" service can be prepared for the evening of the first Sunday of Advent. This is a service where the sanctuary is actually decorated for the Christmas season by the congregation! I have seen as many as one hundred church members attend a rehearsal on the Saturday following Thanksgiving, in careful preparation for this special service. All greenery (silk works best and will last the longest) is laid out on tables, identified with names of those assigned to carry it. Poinsettias and wreaths are on tables. After hot chocolate, cinnamon rolls, and a devotional

thought, responsibility sheets are passed out, listing every group of family or friends and what the responsibility for each group will be. A full explanation is given of what, who, where, why, and when. Then a full "walk-through" of the program, from beginning to end, is conducted. Afterward a question-and-answer period is allowed. Then, and only then, can you be assured your program will come off without a hitch! The service will be glorious and your crowd will be high in attendance because of the numbers of church members you have involved in the service.

The service is integrated with majestic and exciting congregational singing, readings, special solos, choral and instrumental pieces—ending with a short devotional thought from the pastor. It will be a service that your people will want repeated year after year. There are many books available giving full details of how to do a Hanging of the Green service.

• Another evening that will excite your congregation is a service called "The Nine Lessons and Carols." You can find variations on this service from several books in a Christian book store, but the general theme and idea comes from Kings College in England. It is a wonderful time of Scripture readings, congregational singing, processional and recessional, special music, and much, much more—depending on how involved and creative you wish to be with the service.

• And you can also combine "The Nine Lessons and Carols" with "The Hanging of the Green" and have a service that your people will talk about for many weeks to come. It will be a lengthy service—probably an hour and a half—but well worth the effort. Your sanctuary is decorated beautifully while, at the same time, your people are reminded of the beauty of the Christmas story as recorded in Scripture and in music.

- You can take the four morning services and feature separate music groups in each service. Handbells, for instance, can play on congregational hymns, using descant handbell materials available from a variety of music publishers. One such book is entitled *Glad Praises We Ring* (Hymn Accompaniment for Three-Octave Handbells), Van Ness Press, code 4184-13. This book has three Christmas pieces and a variety of other hymns for other seasons.

Instrumental groups can play the prelude, postlude, and/or offertories, in addition to accompanying the anthem or solo.

Recorder groups can play from the narthex, balcony, or be completely unseen, for a prayer response or quiet time.

- Each evening service during the Advent season should be a special "production" service. Feature the children's choirs in one service, the youth choir and youth ensembles and the singles/senior citizens or other ensembles in another service, and select the prime time for the presentation of your church choir and their production for this X-TRA SPECIAL season.

- If your church does the "Singing Christmas Tree," you already have your work cut out for you. One word of caution: Don't let the Singing Christmas Tree become the "tail wagging the dog"! Look carefully at what is happening in your church, at your choir members' lives, and at the time allotment they are giving to this project. Be careful not to expect so much from them that burnout becomes inevitable. There is life in a Christmas season apart from the Singing Christmas Tree—and the congregation has a right to expect more than Singing Christmas Tree emphasis. Look at the amount of time that is being required to bring off a

Singing Tree; look at the creativity of your X-TRA SPECIAL services; and see if there is a good balance for the choirs and the congregation.

• Consider having the lighted bags (bags with sand in the bottom and a candle in the bag) lining the walks to your building at each evening service. (First, check on the local fire code requirements.) The lighted bags will call a great deal of attention to your church from people passing by your facility and will cause conversation in your community. Be sure to have someone in charge of this project. You can't do everything, even though you try! This is a good project for youth, singles, or a men's group—and they will love doing it. In addition to preparation and maintenance, there is clean-up—weekly!

• THE X-TRA SPECIAL season is also a season of sharing your music with the community as a ministry if at all possible. The choir(s), who have worked so hard on their productions, perform their music one time and put it away! Why not find a small, struggling church in your community and have your dress rehearsal in their facility? It will give your choir a lift, an opportunity to perform it once before they perform it at your church, and an uplift to the small church, who will thoroughly enjoy the experience! Consider going to a children's hospital, a senior citizen home, a VA hospital, a prison, or a multitude of other facilities in your city that would welcome a free program from a local church. Your choir will benefit from the ministry experience far more than those to whom you will sing!

Your bell and instrumental group, the youth choir, and other choirs can also minister in your community during this special season and will be welcomed and appreciated. Malls . . . that is another thing entirely! Malls want you to perform, yes! But they don't really care to provide for your performance. All they want is the drawing card of having your choir, bells, or orchestra present a program—to involve people—to entice them to shop. And the noise level, the rude people, the running waters, the crying children—all these do not lend themselves to much "ministry of music." Shy away from mall performances. Be involved in *ministry* performances. These are the people who need you and what you have to offer. Now before you judge too quickly . . . there are exceptions to every situation! Fair enough?

Handbells can draw a crowd anywhere! You know this. Find a unique ministry situation and involve your handbell choir(s) there. Why not secure an invitation to ring at the local Christmas flower show, or whatever is happening near your church that would lend itself to bell playing and the opportunity to minister at the same time! People will love the bells and will stand around and listen far longer than they will for a choir of any kind. Search for the right opportunity and seize it!

So we have taken the opportunity to celebrate the X-TRA SPECIAL season with great joy, excitement, enthusiasm, preparation, and rehearsal. There is such a thing as "planned spontaneity"! Things can seem spontaneous to the congregation that have actually been rehearsed and carefully prepared. These can be high and holy times in the life of your congregation. Prepare them carefully.

Enjoy this X-TRA SPECIAL season to the fullest—every aspect of it. Celebrate the birth of the Lord Jesus Christ in as creative a manner as you can imagine, using all the tools at your disposal—and you and your choirs/groups will enjoy this X-TRA SPECIAL season more than you can ever imagine!

Gloria in Excelsis Deo!

Y
Yahweh

". . . I am who I am . . ." (Ex. 3:14).

God . . . is God. In this Exodus passage, Moses was trying to find out what he was to tell the sons of Israel and was asking God what he should say to them if they questioned his authority. God simply said, "'I AM WHO I AM.' Thus you shall say to the sons of Israel, 'I AM' has sent me to you."

That is simple enough, is it not? That lays it right out there, plain and simple. "I AM." And that should be more than adequate.

How about the call of God in your life? Most musicians do have a definite and personal call from God to serve Him in the area of music and the music ministry. Other musicians simply look upon their job as "choir director" as another job, a position to which to be hired or from which to be fired.

How do you perceive God—YAHWEH—in your music ministry? I am constantly amazed at the number of musicians who do not have a call from YAHWEH in their lives—and yet, these musicians are charged with the responsibilities to provide His music in the worship services of a local church.

Listen to Isaiah 41:9-10,13:
". . . You are my Servant,

I have chosen you and not rejected you.
'Do not fear, for I am with you';
For I am the Lord, your God, who upholds your right hand."

Those are powerful words from YAHWEH Himself. He has called us into our respective ministries with a holy calling. Our responsibilities to Him are immense. This is not a nine-to-five job—this is a ministry to which He has called us. Some people look upon the ministry of music as a "second job," something to supplement the income—and this is acceptable. But this person should be one of high integrity, with a spiritual background; or how can the church assume this person can hold a position of spiritual leadership with spiritual people who love YAHWEH and wish to sing praises to Him through participation in a choir of a local church?

The persons responsible for the music in a church program should spend some amount of time with YAHWEH . . . in His Book . . . in prayer . . . in quietness and solitude as we prepare our rehearsals, our services, our special performances. We should be able to lead the people to YAHWEH on a personal level—both through the group experience and individually. People who are not called by YAHWEH, it seems, would have a most difficult time responding to spiritual things in the context of a service or a rehearsal or with an individual person who comes with a problem or problems. This is not "art" here! This is ministry—music ministry. A director who does not have ministry as one of the callings in his/her life will eventually have trouble dealing with the ministry aspect of the position—for it will appear sooner or later.

Many times, musician ministers are accused of not spending enough time in the Word of God. This may or may not be true. You will have to answer for yourself.

But often people who are doing the accusing are really not aware of the amount of time musician ministers spend in Scripture and prose, researching texts and music to give to their choirs for rehearsal and performance purposes. There is a tremendous amount of Scripture involved in anthem research, which finds its way to the heart as YAHWEH impresses the musician minister to look at this anthem or that anthem.

Great biblical texts are found in anthem after anthem, from the Psalms, from Proverbs—from literally every book in the Bible! For example, these:

"Lord, how long shall the wicked triumph? How long shall they utter and speak hard things? They break in pieces thy people. They slay the widow and the stranger, and murder the fatherless. Yet they say the Lord shall not see. The fear of the Lord is the beginning of wisdom. A good understanding have all they that do His commandments. I will praise Thee, O God. I will sing unto thee among the peoples." ("O Lord God, Unto Whom Vengeance Belongeth," Robert Baker, H. W. Gray, GMCR 1741)

"In His love and in His pity, He redeemed us. In His love and in His pity He provided heaven. Never has another loved us like the Saviour loved. How can anyone suspend himself upon a cross and die for me? Die willingly, to set men free? But He did love. He had pity on us. He provided heaven at last. Shall we not return the favor; live each day for our dear Saviour. And one day He will return for us." ("In His Love and In His Pity," Kurt Kaiser, Word Music, #CS-2966)

"The eyes of all wait upon thee; and thou givest them their meat in due season. Thou openest thine hand, and satisfiest the desire of every living thing." ("The Eyes of All Wait Upon Thee," Gordon Young, Augsburg Publishing House, 11-1264)

"Consider it pure joy, my brothers, whenever you

face trials of many kinds, because you know the testing of your faith develops perseverance." ("Consider It Pure Joy," Bob Burroughs, Kjos Music, GC156)

"All things work together for good to those who love God, to those who are called according to His purpose." ("Song of The Apostle," John Ness Beck, Beckenhorst Press, BP150)

"Where were you when I laid the earth's foundation? Tell me if you understand? Where were you when I marked off its dimensions? Who laid its cornerstone while the morning stars sang together and all the sons of God shouted for joy? Where were you?" ("Where Were You," Ken Barker, Word Music, CS-3001)

"Love is very patient and kind, never boastful or proud; never haughty or selfish or rude; love does not demand its own way; Love is not irritable or touchy. It is never glad about injustice, but rejoices whenever truth wins out." ("Love," Bob Burroughs, Sonshine Productions, SP101)

"A song is a beautiful thing! Voices join in full-throated melody, And life to blend in glorious harmony. Men's hearts are moved, even lifted to ecstasy with a song, for a song is a beautiful thing. But when I sing, Lord, let it not be for this alone, lest fruitless I be when day is done; Touch Thou my lips, Thy beauty let me see, and fill my heart with love eternally, That men may come to know and adore Thee. Lord, this prayer I bring. Lord, for Thee, I sing!" ("Prayer Before Singing," Don Hustad, Hope Publishing Company, HA107)

"You are my portion, O Lord! May Your unfailing love come unto me. I walk about in freedom, for I have seen your face. The earth is filled with your love. May your unfailing love be my comfort. Thy word is a lamp for my feet, and a light for my path. Your compassion is great, O Lord! Blessed are they who walk in the way of the Lord. Alleluia!" ("Psalm 119," David Burroughs, Hinshaw Music, HMC995)

"I will not leave you comfortless. I will come to you yet again: Alleluia! And your heart shall be joyful: Alleluia." ("I Will Not Leave You Comfortless," Titcomb, Carl Fischer, CM441)

"E'en so, I love Thee, and will love, And in Thy praise will sing: Solely because Thou art my God, and my Eternal King!" ("My Eternal King," Jane Marshall, Carl Fischer, CM6752)

There is much spiritual food in these and other songs and anthems . . . some direct quotes from Scripture . . . other allusions to Scripture with powerful messages our people need to hear. It takes time to wade through the musical "junk" that crosses the desk of the music minister to find a few "gems"—musically and textually—that will minister to the spiritual needs of our congregations and our choirs.

But do not interpret what I have just said to mean that the music minister should not spend time in the Word of God. The more time we spend in God's Word, the more effective our ministry will be to our people. It comes in direct portions! You can only minister to your choir members and others as deeply as the Word of God is in your hearts.

Devotional times with our family in the mornings around the table, in the evenings before bedtime . . . personal devotions at the office before the day begins . . . devotions with staff at prearranged times . . . devotional thoughts with our choirs following an exhaustive rehearsal . . . these will enhance the Scriptures and texts studied in preparation for the musical portion of the rehearsals.

Time spent with YAHWEH is time well spent. "I AM WHO I AM."

That says it well, don't you think? We are who we are because YAHWEH is who He is.

Z
Omega

"It is done. I am the Alpha and the Omega, the beginning and the end" (Rev. 21:6).

The end. The finale. The conclusion. The Omega.

Much more could be said under each of the preceding categories than I have said. No doubt you will think of things that should have been said, and maybe some that should have been omitted! But this book was intended to stir some thoughts in your mind, to cause you to dream some dreams, to consider some new ideas, to implement a different way of doing things, to challenge you and your choir(s) to be better than they are, to help choirs know they are accomplishing something great for the kingdom of God through music.

One interesting thing about music: One never tires of it. If you are like most other musicians, on the way home from a good rehearsal, you listen to music via tape, compact disc, or radio. When you are walking on the beach, you are listening to music or making it up in your head as you sing it in your heart. When the weight of the world is heaped upon your shoulders during hours of trial, you probably turn to great music and let it minister to your mind and your heart to ease some of the pain and strain.

Music is a powerful force in the world today. It can

incite mobs to riot frenzy, captivate and tame an angry crowd, minister to the heart of one who is dying of cancer, break the heart of an athlete, melt the heart of a young lady, and pull men and women into the kingdom of God.

Never underestimate music. It is a gift given to us from God, the Father; and it may be the only one of His gifts on earth that we will be able to use in heaven, sharing anew in the resurrection celebration.

Can you imagine singing in a choir of heavenly hosts and heavenly bodies under the direction of J. S. Bach? So you see, dear friends, there is no ending, only a beginning.

God grant you His Spirit.